An Arab Season

Legacy Writings of a Muslim and Christian Relationship

Ms. Pamela

INKWATER PRESS

PORTLAND • OREGON
INKWATERPRESS.COM

This book is dedicated in loving memory
to my parents and grandmother.

Mrs. Marjorie Estelle Williams
Momma, thank you forever for your unconditional love
and support. You epitomized a faithful Christian. I am
deeply hurt and disappointed that you crossed over to
the other side just months shy of my book release that
you were so proudly anticipating – but it was God's will.
Oh how I love and miss you much!
October 16, 1933 – May 5, 2010

Mr. Tommie Lee Williams
Daddy, I kept trying until I got it. I do regret
we did not spend more time together.
Thank you for going with me to father and
daughter camp – I never forgot that day – and
teaching me that a lady crosses her ankles.
I love and miss you.
July 25, 1930 – October 22, 1993

Mrs. Velma Williams
Aunt Bell, thank you for the gumption.
I love and miss you and those jokes.
September 8, 1913 – February 14, 1998

Rolling Back the Souls

I found myself feeling hopeless without a turning point. And now it irrefutably did not matter whether I won or lost.

I only wanted strength to go out fighting with everything I could possibly grasp.

Perhaps dignity was the finale I longed for.

There were a few.

Yes, a few listened and may have understood but, howbeit at every end, I am not satisfied.

So I did what I knew best, prayed.

I thought – who am I?

Who were the ones before me?

My parents, grandparents, great-grandparents, and on and on and on before.

Then it dawned on me to really roll back the souls and meditate on those who prayed and made a way for me.

I cried aloud and pleaded for help from the souls of my ancestors.

Surely they would hear and come.

I knew each soul had given and left something.

Crossing the mighty waters some chose to live and others to die.

The few living kept going for the sake of the many dead.

Another generation was sold, the other toiled and the next soul became relentlessly tired, tired enough to demand change.

Each soul embraced infinite characteristics of the soul before.

The journey of life for each soul may have changed, but what still remained unchanged was that of the soul's purpose.

While rolling back the souls I now could see just what each left for me.

Pride, dignity, impregnability, endurance, beauty, mercy, forgiveness, knowledge, wisdom, long-suffering, tenaciousness, faith, spirituality, and an unimaginable love for the next soul to come, which was me.

Blindly wiping tears, reality stood and addressed my soul.

I indeed am not hopeless.

Remember.

Remember.

Remember from whence I came by rolling back the souls.

For one day, I too, will be a rolled back soul.

What will I have given?

Ms. Pamela
July 1998

Contents

Preface ix

Our Village 1

The Encounter 8

Sundays 17

The First Visit 25

Saturday 39

Friends 48

The Legitimacy of Variation 52

Grandmother's Death 63

A Rose 69

The Secret 74

The School Night Visit 80

Jassem Leaves for Kuwait 83

Jassem's Return 89

The Departure 96

Incidents of Life 103

At The Graveside 113

The Blessing 118

The State Department and the Kuwait Embassy 126

Suspicion 133

First Passage 136
Getting Established.. 139
The Horror of House Cleaning... 146
Truly On Our Own.. 155
Rajean's Death 165
Life in Arizona 168
Marriage.. 173
The Invasion of Kuwait 174
Through the Years.. 176
A Spiritual Moment.. 177
In Thinking.. 180

Preface

A Muslim Kuwaiti officer and I, a Christian African American of Memphis, Tennessee, met in 1978: an unassuming, rich and intimate love grew from this meeting. Our religious and cultural complexities were difficult and at times unacceptable. However, ultimately we graciously acknowledged and respected one another's differences.

The most profound similarity of these two distinctively contrasting faiths is they both embrace the essence of teaching peace and, like the faiths of most other people, a genuine love for one's fellow man.

Despite the personal challenges faced by my dear Muslim friend and me, I remain steadfast that he and the Muslims I have had the privilege to be acquainted with past and current, in the United States and the Middle East, are always loving, giving, culturally astute, and respectful.

Early on the teachings of Christ's inclusive, humbling and loving personality resonated throughout my life. I am persuaded that they framed my heart and mind towards listening and accepting others beyond my religion and race. (Phil. 4:9: Those things, which ye have both learned, and received, and heard, and seen in me, do: and the God of peace shall be with you.)

Furthermore, I am not in any way attempting to condemn one over another (John 3:17: For God sent not His Son into the world to condemn the world; but that the world through him might be saved); instead, to provide some basic knowledge of Muslim and Christian beliefs and practices, and to better inform a few of the culture-phobics.

To this end, I believe unequivocally this journey was predestined and I am inspired to share my legacy writings.

Simply by His grace!

An Arab Season

Our Village

The New Year of 1978 in Memphis, Tennessee, had come and gone two weeks earlier and now, after the first snow has melted, it is briskly cold. Eloise Street in south Memphis, directly off Elvis Presley Boulevard (formerly Bellevue Boulevard), is lined with brick, stone, and wood houses. The well-maintained yards are home to several large families. Our father, Tommie Lee Williams, built our three-bedroom wood-framed home when he married Momma, Marjorie Estelle Jones. I have two older brothers as well as three younger sisters and a younger brother. We have lived all our lives here.

The neighbors call Daddy, "Mr. Tommie Lee." He is a handsome, average height, slender, soft-spoken, reserved man who loves God, his family, and music. Oh how he loves his music! Gospel music is his heart but Daddy also has a noteworthy collection of albums by Louis Armstrong, Fats Domino, B.B. King, and Albert King. For as long as I can remember he held down two or more jobs and for this reason, nice gifts are always under our Christmas tree.

Momma stayed home up until a few years ago when she took on a night job. She is an attractive lady shy of five feet tall, with light hazel-gray eyes. Her very fair skin is due to her biracial mother, a school teacher who passed away early in life. Momma's beauty is natural as evidenced by the photo of her mother, who was a quite striking, regal woman. Very little is spoken about Momma's father and the issue is not pressed. We only know he was an alcoholic who abandoned her and Uncle Joseph, her only sibling, when they were quite young.

In contrast, however, they do speak of her father's mother, "Big Momma," only to say she was a member of the Eastern Star Organization. A small-framed established lady who owned a funeral parlor in Memphis in the early 1900s, she enjoyed traveling the eastern United States and Europe, possibly passing for white. How I would have loved to listen to her stories about life during the Harlem Renaissance and travels to Paris.

Timothy and Marcus, my older brothers, served in the Air Force. Both are married; Marcus resides in Memphis and Timothy in California. At age twenty-two, I am now the oldest at home.

Our small orchard of apple, peach, pear, fig, and persimmon trees satisfies us with pies and fresh delectable fruits in the summer. A small blackberry bush and grapevine provide jarred jellies in the winter. As kids, we played and swung from the apple trees like trained acrobats. We all attended Norris Elementary and Corry Junior High schools in our neighborhood. Mrs. Cooper, the fifth-grade teacher to most of us, Mr. Brown, the principal of the local high school, and a dentist reside on Eloise as well. The majority of the businesses in our community are black-owned and -operated.

Daddy's mother, Aunt Bell, lives next door. She is

the strongest and most independent woman I have ever known. Daddy's first cousins call our grandmother "Aunt Bell." She does not seem to mind us addressing her by this name. Aunt Bell and Granddaddy divorced many years ago and he visits us occasionally. He is a sharply dressed, tall, dark-skinned man with straight coal-black hair, always smoking an odorous fat cigar and handing out one-dollar coins. He wears wide-brimmed hats, two-toned shoes, and tailored long suit coats with a vest pocket watch on which he periodically checks the time. We never understood why Aunt Bell and Granddaddy scrupulously sat in a room for hours on end but no conversation passed between them.

I was never a witness to Aunt Bell's (22-caliber pistol) friend, Roscoe. Marcus knows for a fact it is always at her side in the car under her neatly ironed white mono-grammed handkerchief – no wonder she never allows a soul to touch it. What in the name of life happened to my grandmother that compels her to maintain such a bizarre habit?

Aunt Bell dips light-brown snuff and relaxes by telling us adult mouth-dropping jokes that are incredibly funny. She will laugh so hard it takes her a couple of minutes to gasp for breath. A few times she scared us with this bel-lowing demeanor and we thought Aunt Bell was having a heart attack. Whenever Daddy entered the room and she was telling one of those awful jokes, we all became quiet with guilt-ridden faces and he knew exactly what we were engaged in. Another favorite memory of Aunt Bell is during our summer vacations, when she would enjoy pre-paring her delicious fried chicken wrapped in wax paper as we loaded up in the car to drive north to Detroit to visit relatives.

For over 25 years, Aunt Bell worked at John Gaston Hospital in Memphis, where we were all born. It is hard to imagine she never missed a single day of work.

It is Saturday evening and Momma is engrossed in a telephone conversation, sipping an ice-cold Coca-Cola with the gas oven door ajar to help warm the kitchen. She waves good-bye to me as I put on my coat and go out the side door.

I walk to Thalia Hines's house practically every Saturday evening after bathing to talk or watch television. She is indeed one of my cherished childhood friends. Mrs. Hines, her mom, lives up the street with half her siblings. Thalia and the others live three houses down with their grandmother, Mrs. Clara. No one ever questioned this arrangement and by "southern home training standards" it is considered downright ill-mannered if you do.

On this cold night I hate that I am not able to call Thalia and ask her to open the door. Momma is still on the telephone. Usually I call ahead to tell her I am on my way down. Tonight I agonizingly have to knock and wait. I detest cold weather.

Whenever Thalia greets me at the door, I know instantaneously when she is irritated – a cigarette in her hand and select impious language spews from her mouth.

"Pam, come on in. You know these boys have gotten on my last nerve."

Her two very young nephews live there also. Laughing oftentimes somehow deflates the tense situation. In our home profanity is never spoken, so hearing Thalia is, at best, an innocent and entertaining taboo-break.

She began this path of chain-smoking a few years earlier. After the death of her young niece Tameka, Thalia's nerves permanently frayed. They awakened one night to a fire in the house. As everyone was evacuating, Tameka somehow fell back into a deep sleep and tragically did not escape. The Memphis Fire Department was on strike the night their home burned. The neighbors struggled with tools and water buckets to extinguish the blaze and attempt to save Tameka. Several of them desperately ran across the boulevard yelling and cursing the firemen. The fire department succumbed and eventually dispatched help, but their arrival was too late.

The religious leaders, NAACP, radio stations, and the entire city vehemently condemned this inhumane incident. Especially when everyone learned the fire station was located in "rock throwing" distance directly across the boulevard, and the home with plumes of smoke was in clear view.

Now Thalia's nephews begin a ritual of either being hungry or consistently needing to go to the bathroom when they know we are in the den hanging out. We watch television shows like Amos and Andy or indulge in shameless neighborhood gossip. If they become too impossible, she pulls out a tree switch and dares them to say a mumbling word. Half the time it works and the other half they annoy us.

"Pam, I heard on the radio about this new disco called 2001 at Union and Bellevue on the roof overlooking

Memphis. It costs two dollars to get in before nine. And you know we both need to get out."

"Girl, tell me about it. I only have three dollars to my name and if we get the car from Momma you know I have to put gas in it."

"Pam, Carol gave me a few dollars for babysitting and I will give you two dollars for gas. Ms. Marjorie will not say no if you want to borrow the car. Anyway, I bought a new outfit I want to wear. What are you going to put on?"

"I don't know but, I'll make it cute. Let me see what you bought."

Thalia's closet is near the back door somewhere between the linen and stuff like everyone else on the street with six-plus children – never enough room. She anxiously wants me to see the new beige pantsuit with matching three and one-half inch pumps. It is beautiful with a lace camisole. She holds the outfit to her body and strikes a confident pose against the wall, and we laugh.

"All right now! That's enough!"

We both agree for me to return at eight to pick her up. Most people consider Thalia shy and quiet, but I know her as someone who jokes sarcastically and truly enjoys going out and doing things. I trust her with the most intimate secrets. She attends Lemoyne Owen College as a junior here in Memphis to acquire a degree in accounting.

"Please. Let Momma say yes," I think as I walk up the back porch steps. She is still on the telephone as I walk in. The last thing I want to do is provoke her intense listening. I etch a note on an old brown paper bag and cautiously show it to her. Oh no! This is not good at all. Momma stops talking and places her hand over the receiver.

"You can use the car. Make sure you put gas in it and don't stay out late."

"Yes! Thank you. Thank you."

I am trying my best to get dressed as fast as possible in order to warm the car a few minutes before picking up Thalia. We definitely are styling in the green Duster. I decide to wear a black A-line dress, with black pumps, black fishnet hose, and pinned-up hair as usual. Applying make-up is such a mundane task I can do it blindfolded.

In any case, I want to look extra special going to the new disco and wearing a new maxi coat I received from Daddy for Christmas. After dressing I nonchalantly enter my parents' bedroom to use Momma's Sunday perfume. Before leaving I kiss her and she sniffs rather loudly to suggest she knows I have dabbled in her private stock. She then waves and says be careful.

The Encounter

I have been driving since I was fourteen years old on ice, snow, and in tornado-like weather, and I still refrain from taking foolish chances at any time. Sabrina McGowan, who lived one neighborhood over, died in a car accident one month after receiving her driver's license. We attended the same elementary and junior high schools. How creepy; the day before her death I saw Sabrina at the grocery store and she boasted about being able to go freely here and there. For that very reason alone I envied her something awful.

Poor Sabrina died on impact as she attempted to pass a car on the hill near Forest Hill Cemetery. The bloody wreckage was all over the news. Whenever I feel the urge to pass a vehicle I recall Sabrina's fate.

No surprises this night. After warming the car and backing out the driveway, I see Thalia already stepping off the porch for a curbside pickup.

"Thalia, I think we should buy gas before we go to the disco because you know it will be freezing when we leave. Please, you don't need to say it! I know better than to buy it from the black gas stations out here anyway. I'll wait and get it from one of the white stations closer to the disco where we know it's cheaper."

"You got that right, Pam."

Thalia begins choking on her cigarette and struggling to get a laugh out – gossip is surely on the horizon.

"Okay, Thalia. What's so dog-gone funny? Take me back girl."

"Pam, remember when we were at the Nigerian house party last month? The really tall good-looking guy asked Katrina [one of Thalia's younger sisters] who you were when you started dancing by yourself. I could only understand him say, 'Mun, she dances as though she hasn't a care in the world! Where did she learn to dance like that?' And remember Katrina ticked him off when she said, 'You act like our ancestors ain't from Africa too!' He rolled his eyes and walked away."

"Thalia now you know I can't help it if my dancing is considered slightly exotic. What made you think of that anyway? "

"Girl, I don't know. Maybe because we are going to dance somewhere again," Thalia says, laughing.

Katrina and Stephanie, our younger sisters, are the same age and accompany us on occasion. However, without fail, our outings invariably turn into episodes of their compulsive uncontrolled laughing. With these episodes of embarrassment, we decided to be more selective when those two wanted to tag along. Tonight is one of those nights.

There is one Christmas in particular if I live to be 100 years old I will never forget. When we were teenagers Momma dropped all four of us off down on Beale Street

– better known as the "home of the blues" at the New Daisy Theater to see Blackula, a very low-budget film. This theater house was one of the few in the South to host black movies. I needed to go to the ladies room and when I returned Katrina and Stephanie were laughing hysterically going from one seat to another – almost in a lunatic fashion. I asked Thalia what in the world had happened and she barely could talk for laughing herself. The best I comprehended was the lead vampire had not taken the normal bite from this female victim's neck but instead seductively further down her blouse. As I joined in the innocent humor an animated man walked toward us.

A midget-like usher, with eyes like the movie star Peter Lorre, and a lower lip filled with what appeared to be snuff or chewing tobacco, hurriedly walked down the aisle. He blinded our vision with a large flashlight on our faces. This odd-looking character began scratching his nappy, uncombed salt-and-pepper beard and studied us momentarily while holding up his pants that were either two sizes too large or he didn't have a belt. He authoritatively asked us to stop the disturbance. How could we take him seriously with a high-pitched voice matching his stature? We were motionless but afterwards I slightly eyed him as he exited towards the lobby. All I could see was the back of his tiny head peering from an oversized jacket. We continued snickering.

That incident took second place compared to the next upheaval. This was disastrous from the start. A mouse crawled over my foot and audaciously stopped. It terrified me almost into wetting my clothes. I screamed at the top of my lungs while repeatedly falling down in the folding theater seat. Thalia screamed as well when I shouted about the mouse. Katrina and Stephanie had taken their laughing out to the middle of the aisle. I guess we were now beyond out of control. People stopped watching the movie and began to grumble and stare. The already annoyed usher rushed down and literally "cursed us out" using the worst of all profanity, even as Thalia and I unsuccessfully tried to explain the horror of a mouse during our Christmas outing. He further insulted us by remarking the little harmless rodent had more "upbringing" than we and threatened to escort us from the theater. After what I considered the most embarrassing moment in our lives, we sat on our coats with our feet propped on the seats in front of us. I wanted desperately to call Momma to pick us up early. Unfortunately, this was one of those drop-offs when she was visiting several friends. We had to wait this one out. As usual, we arrived too early and had to sit and watch the silly movie twice.

Momma promptly showed up at ten o'clock. As we were loading in the car, the foul-mouthed usher stepped out with a vile expression on his face. With one hand holding his pants and the other scratching his nasty-looking beard, he stared us down as we drove away.

"Thalia, you know we have a lot of crazy memories. Don't we?"

"Too many if you ask me."

Across from the disco is a Union 76 filling station and gas is less expensive. Tonight it is also crowded – I guess everyone has the same idea. I have to wait almost five minutes for a pump to clear. Thalia hands me two dollars and I step out of the car. I open the gas cap and notice a well-dressed, handsome young man is obviously making his way straight towards me smiling. I turn around to see if he is looking at someone else but apparently not. Too late to pretend I do not see him. Walking closer, I notice his beautiful dark olive complexion and neatly short-trimmed hair. He's probably lost and needs directions. Wearing glasses he appears quite the studious one – he definitely does not look as though he is from Memphis. Out of all the people here tonight, why is he coming towards me?

"Hello!" he said.

"Hi."

"May I pump your gas please?" in a congenial foreign accent.

With a frown I reply, "What?"

"Please. May I pump your gas?"

"No! No! I don't need for you to pump my gas. I can do it myself."

He senses extreme defensiveness and slowly takes a step back.

"Please. I only wanted to pump your gas."

Staring at him and not knowing what to make out of this weird situation.

"I think you better leave me alone," I say in a polite but stern voice.

"No. No. I am sorry. See my friends over there in the car?

I glance for a moment and immediately focus back to him.

"Yeah."

"We are new in town and looking for the 2001 Disco. My name is Jassem. I am trying to be friendly."

I let out a huge sigh of relief and say, "Why didn't you just ask for directions?"

He throws his hands and shoulders up and I shake my head.

"What's your name again?"

"Jassem."

"Well Jassem, look. 2001 is right over there at the top of that building. We are going there too.

"And what's your name?"

"Pam."

We shake hands.

"Pam. Now may I pump your gas for you?"

"No. You really don't need to."

He steps up and slowly reaches for the nozzle as I back away.

"I was trying to be pleasant and did not wish to scare you. You looked friendly and we needed directions."

"Well Jassem, you scared me anyway."

Slightly laughing he said, "Oh. I am very sorry. Please forgive me, Pam. Please get back in your car. I will take care of this."

I attempt to give him the two dollars and he refuses, insisting I get inside the warm car.

"Don't worry, I will take care of it."

"Thank you."

Thalia says she heard it all as I hand her back the money.

"Thalia, I can hardly understand him. He is some kind of foreigner and paying an absolute stranger's gas."

"Hmm! He's a fine foreigner."

"Girl don't you think this is kind of weird? Yes. I will

give him that. He is fine but I don't know. What should we do?"

"Pam I think it's alright."

"You are probably right."

There is a peck on the glass and it is the generous stranger, Jassem.

"Would it be okay if we follow you over?"

"Sure. And thanks again for buying the gas."

He smiles and rushes to his car. Starting the car, Thalia and I notice a full tank of gas. I am speechless.

The disco parking lot is full but we manage to locate a couple of spaces. We barely understand their English as Jassem introduces Thalia and me to his two companions, Latif and Nedal. We have to enter two double doors inside the building and signs point to elevators up to 2001. There are so many people stepping into the elevator we wait for the next one. The music becomes louder and louder as we arrive at the top. Everyone is quiet with anticipation. When the elevator door finally opens, smoke, disco lights, loud bass music, and happy conversing people fill the hallway. There are three bouncers and two guys selling the tickets and stamping hands as we turn to the right towards the disco entrance. Jassem gestures no as I reach to pay. Thalia and I graciously thank him. This is an unusual custom but how refreshing. The club is too crowded to enter. We locate a booth in the restaurant on the opposite side. Thalia is on the inside, I sit in the middle, and Jassem on the end. It is a spectacular view as the top floor slowly revolves. I had no idea Memphis is so beautiful at night. I feel Jassem's eyes on me the entire time and do not know what to make of it. Everyone orders Cokes.

He and his friends appear very well maintained and are noticeably polite.

"So Jassem, where is your home?"

"Kuwait."

"Where?"

"Kuwait. It is in the Middle East."

"Wow! I have never heard of that place before. What are you doing in America?"

"We are in the Kuwait Air Force and stationed at Millington Naval Air Station for training. Where are you from?"

"I was born and raised right here in good ole Memphis Tennessee."

Thalia starts bobbing her head and says, "Pam girl, there is your song."

"Pam, would you like to dance?" asks Jassem.

"Sure!"

Jassem takes my hand and he literally shoves our way onto the center of the dance floor. Everyone is eager to dance to the popular song playing, "More Than a Woman" by the Bee Gees. We barely have enough room to maneuver. I am shocked to hear Jassem singing the song, especially with his heavy accent.

"I love this song by the Bee Gees. How do you know it?"

That is probably an ignorant question. I assumed he only listened to his native music. He does not answer but instead laughs and keeps dancing and singing. We dance and dance almost the entire night especially since the disc jockey is playing all the hit songs from the new movie, Saturday Night Fever. We both are drenched in sweat from dancing and I need to dry off before going out so as not to catch a death of cold. Everyone is enjoying the evening and engaging in small talk to pass the time until we dry off a bit.

"Thalia, what time is it?"

"It's almost twelve-thirty."

"Yeah. It's time to go."

Jassem and his friends also decide to leave when we leave. While waiting for the elevator, we see people coming in after midnight. I take the keys out and walk to the car. Jassem politely opens the door. When I thank him for everything, he asks for my telephone number. I have no reservations giving my number to him. Jassem asks if he could call me tomorrow and if so, what would be a good time. I suggest after three. He asks if I live far from where we are and I explain it is a few miles straight south down Elvis Presley Boulevard. Jassem reaches into his pocket, pulls out a wrinkled receipt, and I write the number on it. Afterwards, I drive away.

"Pam, aren't you glad we came here tonight? That was fun! And I am going to say it. Now those are some goo-o-d-looking men! You cannot tell me Jassem was not checking you out all night girl."

"He does have a nice smile and beautiful teeth to go with it, Thalia. Where the heck is Kuwait?"

"Don't ask me. I have never heard of the place before."

"Tomorrow I am going to look for Kuwait in the encyclopedia."

Sundays

Sunday is unquestionably the Lord's Day in our home – on our street for that matter. Daddy is awake before the crack-of-dawn and occupies our one bathroom for at least an hour, leaving Momma and the rest of the entire family often less than one hour and a half of preparation for worship. He crafted an oversized wood shelf above the toilet for towels and toiletries with hooks fixed on the side to hang his AM/FM radio. Daddy's love for worship and music caused him every Sunday morning to wake the house by the blasting of radio station WDIA. It probably is pride. WDIA is the first black station to air in the country. Preaching and gospel music air all day Sunday.

Thinking back, right before leaving for service, Daddy would call us all in his bedroom and give us money for offeringeven when we took on part-time minuscule jobs. He would always ask if we had anything to tithe. He pulled his chair up to a large wooden homemade safe secured with a regular lock that kept money, pictures, important papers, and reel-to-reel gospel sermons.

Years of practice perfected my parents, three brothers and three sisters to be suited, shoes shined, faces and knees oiled up, teeth brushed, and dressed for morning

Bible class by ten. One by one, we patiently hung out in the living and dining room until the last one was ready and then piled in the station wagon. We took turns looking through our black iron glass front door at the neighbors leaving, and waving if we got their attention. The Holmes are Methodist, the Gardners Baptist, and Thalia's family is Pentecostal.

The Babcocks, who live on the corner across the street from Thalia, are members of the Church of Christ also. They attend one of the congregations nearby. Brother and Sister Babcock's business is also on their property. It is a malt stand where a dime can buy three large sweet lemon cookies and a delicious vanilla or chocolate ice cream cone. Everyone knows about Brother Babcock and some deep backwater-rooted superstition concerning washing his cars. Literally years layered with grit and grime coat his cars. When he drives up the street to visit his sister you hear some elderly person make a point by saying, "That's a sin and shame before God. And that don't make no sense at all. And he calls himself a Christian."

The best Sunday mornings are those when Aunt Bell walks down her back porch to the wire fence that separates our properties and yells out for one of us to meet her. She hands the most mouth-watering yeast biscuits ever made to whoever races and makes it there first. A square flat cast-iron skillet holds a couple of dozen covered completely with a potato sack dish towel. In a stern but harmless voice, she cautions, "Don't you drop 'em now."

Preparation for these biscuits was indeed a two-day process. Beginning on Friday until Sunday morning, the dough remained at room temperature to rise for baking.

Those yeast biscuits dipped in pure butter and our home-made grape jelly are a breakfast fit for royalty.

It is imperative that our family leave on time for morning worship service. Finding a parking space is difficult due to members arriving from all over the city. Depending on how much time we had to get there, Daddy would rotate one of three different routes through Memphis.

As young children when we arrived at church, one of my brothers without fail, usually Marcus, would break out running and Daddy immediately would say, in his no-nonsense, listen-to-me voice, "Do not run. Walk! Walk! That church ain't going nowhere."

Our congregation is located downtown a couple of miles from Beale Street. The original church structure is a small red-brick building with a large old magnolia tree in front. As we enter for morning worship, the brilliant sun shines through the stained-glass windows, striking the burgundy pews and carpet. The song leader begins with a hymn and the magnificent melodious a cappella singing follows. How Great Thou Art!

Due to rapid growth, an expansion of our building was needed. However, it lacked the character of the old building, which classrooms and a dining hall now occupy. Perhaps modern architecture and accommodating of hundreds of members did not mesh well. Membership had increased at least four-fold during that time and we were the largest black Church of Christ in the country. Steady growth moved the congregation to the current location in south Memphis.

The entire group of elders and deacons would sit on the platform until our minister, Brother Nicolaus Lambert, stepped to the podium to begin his sermon. He is well known and respected throughout the brotherhood with a Sunday afternoon broadcast on WDIA and through the week in South Africa.

The Lord's Supper, also referred to as Communion, is observed every Sunday. It is a weekly table of remembrance that Christ died for our sins. From the Holy Bible, Luke 22:14–19: And when the hour was come, he sat down, and the twelve apostles with him. And he said unto them, With desire I have desired to eat this passover with you before I suffer: For I say unto you, I will not any more eat thereof, until it be fulfilled in the kingdom of God. And he took the cup, and gave thanks, and said, Take this, and divide it among yourselves: For I say unto you, I will not drink of the fruit of the vine, until the kingdom of God shall come. And he took bread, and gave thanks, and brake it, and gave unto them, saying, This is my body which is given for you: this do in remembrance of me.

Acts 20:7: And upon the first day of the week, when the disciples came together to break bread, Paul preached unto them, ready to depart on the morrow; and continued his speech until midnight.

If for any reason one of the men or young boys during this segment of worship is not considered "appropriately" dressed (wearing a suit coat or jacket), temporary attire is provided from a storage closet. Service is formal and orderly.

After worship, you witness an array of well-dressed black folk from all over Memphis. Some bourgeoisie, other families from the surrounding public housing, and blue- and white-collar workers unite as members of one large church family. In the spring women parade their matching frocks, hats, and gloves and the girls are meticulously dressed with petticoats, patent leather shoes, and perfectly hot-combed hair. Yes, these proud black men are Christians and some of the brethren even have the audacity to sway in their stepping.

When I was a little girl I remember asking Daddy, why do men wear hats all the time? He smiled and said, "Pamela Jean, a man without a hat is like a man not having any shoes on." For many years following when I noticed a man not wearing a hat, I immediately looked down at his feet.

Stephanie and I often would go to the grocery store across the street from church and buy a large dill pickle topped with a long peppermint in the middle to tide us over until dinner. On those seriously extended morning services, mostly funerals, I would buy a hot dog with pickles and coleslaw – what a delicious snack. Church members made their way into the store purchasing last-minute dinner items.

Momma prepares Sunday's meat the night before because we're famished after worship. When it is time for Daddy to bless the food, no one dares be anywhere or doing anything else. From time to time, we invite friends from church for dinner. Stephanie and I are the unofficial sweep-and-dishwashing crew. After dinner, a Sunday ritual ensues: Momma in the bedroom reading the newspaper until she dozes off, Daddy stretched out on the living room couch listening to sermons or his gospel albums, and everyone else heading out.

Most "gospel meetings" or "revivals," as they are called,

start on Sunday at different congregations throughout Memphis and neighboring cities south of Memphis, including over the state line in Mississippi. Daddy consistently asks if I want to go with him. He knows I will say yes. When we arrive at the church he finds a seat near the front and I usually sit with anyone who appears warm-hearted or has children that look friendly. At these revivals, the singing is so soul stirring, it makes you weep with joy and is heard throughout the neighborhood. An abundance of "Amen" outbursts is heard when the minister strikes those spiritual chords.

In north Memphis, one church in particular is across the street from "Uncle Charlie's" corner malt store. Now, who can say if this man is related to us, or if he is everyone's uncle? Daddy and I walk over after the revival and socialize briefly. Uncle Charlie, being the gracious owner, offers to fry a quick burger or hot dog and Daddy always refuses. However, I accept the candy or cookies of my choosing.

Each summer we drive to Mobile, Alabama, to visit our dear friends, the Whitakers. Brother Whitaker is a minister and he and his wife too have a large family. We leave Saturday morning and upon arrival in the afternoon we are welcomed with loving outstretched arms. Their home is nestled on several acres of land with an apparently endless garden. Corn is everywhere and there is a small smokehouse. The carport has comfortable, neatly arranged lawn chairs where the adults can relax and take in the country air away from the heat and sun. These two families of children play and roam for hours and sometimes stay out way past dark catching lightning bugs and frogs in jars. At night blankets, cots, sofa sleepers, and anything possible to sleep on cover every space throughout their lovely home.

Momma and Sister Whitaker are the closest of friends. They are in the kitchen at dawn preparing biscuits, eggs, home-made jelly, and smoked ham. Everyone leaves for morning worship with full stomachs.

Brother Whitaker's congregation is located around the corner within walking distance from their home. A very small, white, wood-framed old country building with a cross erected on top, the church is supported by large brick sections and you can see under the building from the front to the back. The parking lot is not paved like our congregation at home so people drive in slowly so the dust does not stir up. Despite it not being modernized outside, it is clean and comfortable inside. The back and front doors of the building remain open during service and the smell of cattle is ever present. The church members greet and hug us as though we are kin. All the women and children are seated on the left and the young adult and older men sit together on the right towards the front.

Momma consciously reminds us to use the bathroom before we leave because the church only has an outhouse. It looks as though it has been around for decades. The boys think of using it as an adventure but I always imagine falling in and dying.

Sunday dinner is literally enough food to feed a small army. Everyone gathers in the dining and living room for Brother Whitaker to bless the food. Turkey, dressing, fried chicken, fresh shucked corn, okra, collard greens, sweet tomatoes, yams, cornbread, potato salad, sweet potato pies, and the sweetest iced tea decorate the formal table.

We normally leave for home a couple of hours after dinner and clean-up. Sister Whitaker loads Momma's arms with fresh snap peas, collard and turnip greens, white corn, and tomatoes from her garden. Daddy meticulously packs the vegetables in the back as we without hurry load the car. The entire family stands in the front waving until we are out of sight.

Driving home the car is silent with sadness. All you hear is the breeze from the wind as it blows on our faces in the rear seats of the station wagon.

Oh how I immensely enjoy visiting the Whitakers.

The First Visit

Stephanie and I had cleaned the dining room and kitchen after Sunday dinner. Normally I take a two-hour nap but not today. I want to be certain not to miss Jassem's call. I stretch across the bed with the telephone to my ear to relax a bit. Before long, I fall into a deep sleep.

"Answer the phone. Would someone please answer the phone?" Momma shouts.

The nap had turned into a hard hour-and-a-half rest and I had not heard the phone ringing. As I arise, the telephone falls to the floor.

"What is going on?"

"I got it, Momma!" as I fumble to pick it up.

"Hello! Speaking."

It is Jassem and I sound completely out of breath. He apologizes for awakening me. He admits to sleeping in and studying with some of his friends. One of his colleagues lives off base and prepared dinner for everyone. Jassem returned to his room to call me and see if he can visit. I give him directions to our home and my estimation is he will arrive in about thirty to forty-five minutes.

Our glass front door reveals everything on the

hardwood floors, so I take the dust mop to make certain not a crumb is present. Our family has a reputation for having a meticulously clean home. So, I nervously wipe down the kitchen with bleach but forget to dilute it with water. I am feverishly attempting to rid the front of the house of the lingering if not toxic scent by waving the dishtowel back and forth. I want to open the door but Daddy will have a conniption fit if I do that with the heater on.

"Who is that with all the Clorox?" asks Daddy while lying on the couch.

"Me. I was cleaning the kitchen. Daddy, it was an accident."

Melinda, one of my younger sisters, runs up the hall and facetiously makes matters worse by pretending to choke.

"I don't know why she had to use so much!" Melinda says sarcastically. "I can't breathe!"

Deciding not to dignify her with any response, I go into the bathroom and freshen up.

Jassem arrives an hour later with a friend. When he speaks, it makes me want to listen to him even more.

"Pam. This is Nuri."

"Hello."

I introduce Jassem and Nuri to Daddy. Daddy looks at them briefly and goes into the kitchen. There is an awkward moment of silence.

"Pam, you look beautiful and your father seems very strict," says Jassem.

"Thank you, Jassem. My Daddy will not seem strict as you say once you get to know him. Would you or Nuri care for some water or something to drink? I think we have some Coke."

They both answer, "No, thank you."

"So Jassem, what's your last name?"

"Al-Hashash. Jassem Ahmed Al-Hashash."

"Everyone calls me Pam but my name is Pamela. Pamela Williams. What is your last name, Nuri?

"Hussein."

"So tell me, Jassem, how long have you been in this country and why are you here?"

"I have been in the states for one year and in Millington one month. I am studying maintenance on the F-14 and F-15 planes."

"You are interested in fighter planes."

"Yes. So I can return home and teach."

Nuri and Jassem have been friends for many years. Nuri is a slender man, six feet plus inches tall with emerald-green eyes. I ask him about this unusual trait and he replies that his East Indian mother graced him with the eyes.

Jassem and his friends are all officers in the Kuwait Air Force. He is a Second Lieutenant and Nuri is a Captain. They both speak several languages and besides English, Jassem speaks fluent French, Italian, and some Russian. On the base, they reside at the Bachelor Officers Quarters, also referred to as the BOQ.

I am in awe of his knowledge of American History. He speaks of the assassination of Dr. Martin Luther King Jr. and wants to eventually visit the Lorraine Hotel in Memphis to see where it actually took place. I tell him and

Nuri about an unforgettable experience I endured during that time.

Mrs. Winifred, another one of Momma's close friends, telephoned our home with the news of Dr. King's assassination. All I heard was Momma screaming and running out the front door. The neighbors had taken to the streets and there was crying, confusion, and utter disbelief. Daddy arrived shortly after the phone call to see if Momma had heard. Carloads of men were en route downtown to the Lorraine Hotel. Neighbors talked under the streetlights all through the night. Memphis was under a dusk-to-dawn curfew because of the rioting and chaos. The National Guard was called upon to enforce the curfew. I did not know much at all about Dr. Martin Luther King. I simply drew the conclusion that this man was very special to blacks and he was now dead.

During the curfew, I took no thought about walking down to Thalia's one night as I normally did. As I hurried down the street two National Guardsmen pulled up in a Jeep unexpectedly. They frightened me to death and one shouted in a harsh voice, "Where are you going?"

I tried to explain I was on my way to Thalia's home. One of them told me to turn around quickly and go back. I became afraid of being in serious trouble not only with them but also with my parents. As I started walking up the back porch, Momma opened the door and asked me what was I doing outside and told me not to do it again. I am thankful to God Daddy did not witness them stopping me. The incident could have seriously angered him and others, which might have resulted in an unpleasant set of circumstances.

During this tumultuous time, everyone was transfixed to the radio because of the curfew. WDIA announced business was as usual in the white neighborhoods in east Memphis and even went as far as naming those businesses. The filthy stench of racism permeated the city. This only infuriated people especially when everyone was urged to keep calm and not violate the curfew, risking arrest. Quite a few Memphians did not stand for it and blatantly disregarded the curfew, resulting in their arrests. The rioting slowly concluded but hostility and uncertainty followed many weeks after.

Even with the Memphis sanitation workers strike, the water hosing of people, and the murder of Dr. Martin Luther King, not one word of racism or racist remarks found its way into our home. Yes, we naturally identified if a person was black or white but absolutely nothing beyond that.

I also remember Daddy taking the entire family to the downtown Malco Theater one Saturday evening to see The Ten Commandments. As our family entered we were politely guided upstairs to the balcony for blacks while the whites sat downstairs. Despite the injustices we inherited from society, as a family we are gifted and blessed with love and spirituality. That evening was one of the best family outings I remember.

My conclusion is God lives in the hearts and souls of Daddy, Momma, and Aunt Bell. And I assume they never made racial comments to us because the lesson to learn is God is larger than man's social ills and the Williams children eventually would discover this dichotomy of life on their own.

Jassem is telling me about his home, Kuwait, a tiny place almost unnoticeable on the map, and the other surrounding countries in the Middle East. He has two sisters and one brother and is the youngest sibling. He is a Muslim and I am curious about this foreign religion. Perhaps he might consider going to church with me in the future to experience how I worship God. Nuri takes cigarette breaks several times on the porch while observing the neighborhood. I cannot determine if he feels uncomfortable or is completely bored listening to Jassem and me go on. Momma finally awakens from her nap and walks up the hall.

"Momma, this is Jassem and Nuri. I met Jassem last night when Thalia and I went out. They are from the Middle East."

Momma looked at the both of them and asked, "Now how do you pronounce your names?"

"Jassem."

"Nuri."

"Well, Jassem and Nuri, nice to meet you. The both of you young men are certainly far away from your homes. Now tell me, what brings you to Memphis?"

Jassem, with Nuri's help, begins explaining to Momma why they are in the States and provides a one-minute history lesson on Kuwait. It is apparent at times the accent is difficult.

"Again, it is nice to meet you and I hope to see you young men again."

As Momma leaves the room she reminds me it is almost time for evening worship service.

"Jassem, I need to get ready and go back to church. I'm glad you and Nuri came by to see me."

They begin speaking in Arabic and I politely wait for them to finish. Nuri is explaining or making a point to Jassem. Listening to the tones of their voices and observing their gestures, I say, "You want to come back?"

Jassem and Nuri abruptly stop and peer at me in total disbelief, speaking again in Arabic to each other.

"Pam, how did you know what we were talking about?" questions Jassem.

"I don't know. I guess I read your hands and face."

Nuri smiles and says, "Unbelievable. Unbelievable."

Jassem wants to return later and take me to the movies. He will return around eight o'clock and I am going to search the newspaper for a show. I am surprised he does not mind driving back and forth from Millington.

When Jassem and Nuri leave I can hardly contain myself to show Momma in the encyclopedia where they actually live on the map. She also had noticed their polite mannerisms and wondered how I understood a word either one of them said.

Aunt Bell telephones and wants me to ride with her to church. She works on Sunday mornings and only attends evening worship. I have to be on time. She is known for leaving anyone not promptly waiting at the edge of the drive when it is time to leave. Riding with her requires solid nerves. She drives as though rocks are tied to her shoes whenever she has to stop or go, not to mention her continual joking. How she ever avoided getting tickets for running red lights is a complete mystery. By God's grace, I am certain.

Tonight my sisters and I decide to sit with her. Worship ends at seven o'clock promptly. Aunt Bell is never rude towards church members and for that matter, neither is she sociable – another one of those idiosyncratic curses.

Driving onto Eloise I do not see Jassem's car and a joyous sigh of relief follows. Whoever rides with Aunt Bell has to get out and open her gate. Her home is on a slight hill and as soon as she approaches the drive, she immediately steps on the gas and stops abruptly when she reaches the top. My goodness! We all fear her skills will be slightly off one day and she will end up hitting the persimmon tree on the other end of the drive. Her legs are starting to give her trouble and she appreciates when we close the gate. I wave good-bye and go into the house.

On Sunday evenings we eat leftovers and watch television. Tonight is no different. I warm a serving of egg custard pie while impatiently looking out the dining room window. Finally! Jassem drives up in his blue-and-white 1977 Cutlass. I expected Nuri but Jassem is alone. As I open the front door, the expressions on both of our faces mirror our eagerness to see one another again. Nuri decided to remain on base and I have the feeling his role is Jassem's "big brother." Perhaps as close friends and foreigners here not knowing what to expect, Nuri possibly needed to give his approval.

While searching the paper for a movie I notice an unusual key-chain he placed on the dining room table.

"This is odd. What is it?"

"Remember, I am Muslim. This represents Islam. As your cross represents Christianity."

After searching the entertainment section we both want to see Saturday Night Fever and it starts at nine o'clock. I usually don't take in a movie late in the evening. This is, however, an exception. As Jassem opens my door, I pick up a book from the seat and place it on the floor. It is his Qur'an.

"No! No! Please don't put this book on the floor. This is my Qur'an," he says in a pleasant but serious tone as he picks it off the floor and places it on the back seat. I feel I did something terribly wrong.

"Jassem, I am sorry. What is it?"

"Christians live by the Bible and Muslims live by this Qur'an. Do not worry about it. You didn't know."

He senses I feel awful as he closes the door. Does his religion require him to treat this book with such regard, or is he simply oversensitive? Maybe I handled something of his carelessly?

"Jassem, may I see it please?"

"Sure, Pam."

Skimming through his Qur'an makes no sense to me. It is entirely in another language, Arabic.

"Pam. It's okay. Please be happy, relax and let's enjoy the evening."

"Jassem, there are two things I want you to do."

"What?"

"First, tell me about your Qur'an sometime. Secondly, heat please. I am freezing!"

"I can do both," he says, and we start laughing.

He turns on his eight-track and "More Than a Woman" by the Bee Gees starts playing – undoubtedly he planned this perfectly. Jassem cannot hold one note but this does not deter him from pretending to be a singer.

I am an old fan of the Bee Gees. As part of the Memphis City Schools integration efforts, Stephanie and I were bused to Overton High in east Memphis. I met an extraordinary white guy by the name of Chad. He never said it but I suspect he thought it was rather "hip" to have a black female friend. Underneath Chad's long auburn "hippie-like" hair was a handsome and highly intelligent person. We had become comfortable talking about mostly anything. I had the biggest crush on him but it would have ruined our friendship had I told him. Chad smoked marijuana and he knew I was aware of this little vice. He never offered or smoked in my presence. He probably had a bigger crush on me than I had on him. It was easy listening to Chad educate me on his enjoyment of British artists and rock music. We would go out to midtown at a quaint piano bar in Overton Square. I found appreciation for these new music genres. Thus, my eclectic taste in music evolved once again. Elton John, the Bee Gees, and Peter Frampton became personal favorites for many years. Chad in turn listened and enjoyed the soulful melodies of Harold Melvin and the Blue Notes, S.O.S., Dramatics, Temptations, and local Memphis artists Isaac Hayes, Al Green, the Bar-Kays, and the Temprees.

As Jassem drives south from Eloise Street down the boulevard we enter a community of Memphis called Whitehaven where Graceland (Elvis Presley's home) is located. Whitehaven was an exclusive white neighborhood up until a few years ago. Jassem never imagined how close this tourist attraction is to our home. Fans and on-lookers are always present any hour of the day or night taking pictures and peering through the large white gates at the entrance of the estate. It was not uncommon to see Elvis and his wife, Priscilla, out in the area when I was a little girl. It also held true how generous and compassionate he was towards people. Before Elvis became so famous, he spent a considerable amount of time hanging out with the black musicians down on Beale Street. I heard this is where he learned all about the down-home blues and developed his legendary moves.

After a few minutes of Jassem's gawking, we then take the interstate downtown to Beale Street. You can hear blues playing before we make it to the main strip. The gaiety of people is everywhere. We head farther west to Front Street, which faces the Mississippi River. Old blighted factory buildings are being converted into exclusive lofts, condominiums, and expensive eateries. The reflection of the West Memphis Arkansas Bridge on the water is surreal. It begins snowing and Jassem is too new to the area to feel safe enough driving through town. So we agree to make the movie some other night. I have a part-time job which starts early tomorrow morning and I need to study for my evening classes at Shelby State Community College.

As he parks in the driveway I thank him for the evening and he in turn thanks me for seeing him again. Jassem walks me to the door and asks if he can call me tomorrow. I say yes. He then kisses my hand and leaves.

While preparing for bed I reflect on the incident surrounding his Qur'an. Is this my first lesson in handling the Qur'an? Time will reveal this enigma. Jassem is refreshingly different and unlike anyone I know. I seem completely drawn to this handsome and very interesting stranger. I wonder what he thinks about my belief in our Lord and Savior, Jesus Christ?

Islam

Allah is the Arabic word for God. A Muslim is one who follows Islam. The Qur'an is a complete and original compilation of the Final Revelation from God to mankind through the last Prophet, Muhammad (peace be upon him). Muslims submit to the will of God and accept the Prophet Muhammad (peace be upon him) as his last messenger. Also, it contains earlier Revelations made to Jesus, Abraham, David, and Moses. The Qur'an instructs Muslims how to worship God, respect other faiths and care for their loved ones, the poor, needy, and orphans. Islam places significance on peace. Qu'ran 41:34: Nor can Goodness and Evil be equal. Repel (Evil) with what is better: then will he between whom and you was hatred, become as it were your friend and intimate!

The crescent moon and star is an internationally recognized symbol of the faith of Islam. These two symbols actually pre-date Islam by several thousand years. Legend holds that the founder of the Ottoman Empire, Osman, had a dream in which the crescent moon stretched from one end of the earth to the other. Taking this as a good omen, he chose to keep the crescent and make it the symbol of his dynasty. The symbol is featured on the flags of several Muslim countries. Finally, according to popular tradition, whenever the Prophet Muhammad (peace be upon him) first caught sight of a new moon he would say:

"Oh crescent moon of good and guidance, my faith is in Him who created you!"

Christianity – The Cross

John 19:17-30: And he bearing his cross went forth into a place called the place of a skull, which is called in the Hebrew Golgotha: Where they crucified him, and two other with him, on either side one, and Jesus in the midst. And Pilate wrote a title, and put it on the cross. And the writing was, JESUS OF NAZARETH THE KING OF THE JEWS. This title then read many of the Jews: for the place where Jesus was crucified was nigh to the city: and it was written in Hebrew, and Greek, and Latin. Then said the chief priests of the Jews to Pilate, Write not, The King of the Jews; but that he said, I am King of the Jews. Pilate answered, What I have written I have written. Then the soldiers, when they had crucified Jesus, took his garments, and made four parts, to every soldier a part; and also his coat: now the coat was without seam, woven from the top throughout. They said therefore among themselves, Let us not rend it, but cast lots for it, whose it shall be: that the scripture might be fulfilled, which saith, They parted my raiment among them, and for my vesture they did cast lots. These things therefore the soldiers did. Now there stood by the cross of Jesus his mother, and his mother's sister, Mary the wife of Cleophas, and Mary Magdalene. When Jesus therefore saw his mother, and the disciple standing by, whom he loved, he saith unto his mother, Woman, behold thy son! Then saith he to the disciple, Behold thy mother! And from that hour that disciple took her unto his own home. After this, Jesus knowing that all things were now accomplished, that the scripture might be fulfilled, saith, I thirst. Now there was set a vessel full of vinegar: and they filled a sponge with vinegar, and put it upon hyssop, and put it to his mouth. When Jesus therefore had received the vinegar, he said, It is finished: and he bowed his head, and gave up the ghost.

Saturday

A little over two weeks and Jassem and I have either seen or talked to one another every day – even with all the studying between us. He respects me and one of his best qualities is how genuine he is. He shares with me the places all around the world he has gone. I am intrigued to discuss places I only read about in high school. Jassem admitted that ever since he began traveling away from home he had been homesick for Kuwait but since we've met he doesn't miss it as much.

Typical Saturday ensues as normal with Daddy in the driveway washing his car and Momma at the hairdresser. My sisters are relaxing in the back room watching television. Jassem is picking me up around two o'clock to grab a bite to eat and see the long-awaited movie Saturday Night Fever.

The window above the sink is ajar and I hear someone walking softly up the back porch steps. It is my eccentric cousin, Rajean. She has a perfect round face with mocha skin and elegant mannerisms. She adorns her head with wraps and sports dashiki tops, along with oversized shoulder bags or a backpack. By all accounts a borderline genius who spends a notable amount of time at the library and oddly a high school dropout, which no one could fathom.

Rajean is tremendously misunderstood, which accounts for the moments of sadness her spirit mirrors. In retrospect, she should have attended an elitist institute to develop those extraordinary true gifts. At times, her articulate conversation is so incomprehensible I become completely lost in it but constantly listening anyway in hopes of learning something. She nevertheless put the fear of God in me when she spoke solemnly of the United States one day coming under attack either by internal or external forces. At times, she insists I take her seriously and adamantly believes in having survival gear ready at a moment's notice. There is a camping store in our neighborhood that Rajean often visits. She maintains supplies and told me eventually of her goal to relocate to higher ground in the mountains. What mountains? What was she internalizing during those long hours at the library or who knows where else? What did she hear to arrive at such an abstruse conclusion? Whether I believed her or not, it sounded credible enough, so I always gave her the utmost attention.

Whenever I feel poorly, Rajean the healer would educate me on specific herbs to make me feel better and cure my common ailments. She also kept a small canister of snuff for minor cuts or abrasions; truth to this, Aunt Bell taught her this remedy. She invites me often to go to a health food store in midtown that sells natural products but I am not yet interested. Nonetheless, she is astutely contrary. Normal people sit and you serve them, not Rajean. In a melodramatic manner she pulls out a small brown paper bag of loose leaf tea, a mini-sieve, and a miniature jar of honey. She only requires a cup of hot water. Whatever the subject matter, she knows a little about everything, which in itself is astonishing.

"Hey Pam. What's up?"

"Hey Rajean. What are you up to?"

"Okay. Spill the beans. What is this I hear about you and some Arab?"

"Our family needs stock in Western Union. Good grief!"

I am anxious to talk about Jassem and Kuwait. I thought, finally I know something I can teach her. Well, here we go again! She tells me some of the same things Jassem has shared with me about this tiny Arab country. Rajean recalls having a Qur'an in her possession and will bring it over as soon as she locates it. Rajean considered converting to Islam years ago but I did not bother to ask why she changed her mind. What would Jassem think of Rajean giving me a Qur'an? She further explained Kuwait is one of the most westernized Arab countries. Women attend co-ed universities and hold certain positions opting to wearing the traditional black burqa or non-traditional dress. Most other Muslim countries are extremely traditional or conservative in regards to women and their roles.

She strongly suggests I be aware of all aspects of Islam, in respect to the relationships of men and women, and specifically the potential involvement with Jassem. During her brief Rajean "101" she alludes several times to me not becoming offended, but that I should be cognizant of the fact he is a foreign national on soil where particular freedoms are currently at his disposal – suggesting I observe him. She leaves after having some tea and most assuredly I take her advice to heart. Our conversation places me a tad behind schedule.

I have a hair appointment at one o'clock that will take at least an hour. Walking hurriedly out the drive, I tell Daddy where I am going in the event Jassem arrives. Mrs. Atkins, my beautician, lives up the street and conducts business from her kitchen. The Atkins family never had children and always kept a pet. Tiny, a Chihuahua, is her latest child with rolls of fat, like a newborn baby. Mrs. Atkins handles a straightening comb and marcelle irons as though the inventor, Madam C. J. Walker, created them for her hands. The fee is two dollars to press and another two for curling. I had cried so much when Momma pressed my hair – when Mrs. Atkins took me on as a client it was a relaxing "put you to sleep" experience. She never burned me once. Today, Mrs. Atkins must have read my mind by asking if I had any plans. I hinted about the two o'clock date and she finished in forty-five minutes. As I stretched rising from the chair she smiled and said with a singing tone, "mo hair."

Walking back towards home I do not see Jassem's car. This means I probably have time to take a quick duck bath. I have barely started filling the tub when I hear Daddy speaking to someone. It must be Jassem and on time of course. Felton, my younger brother, answers the door and introduces himself.

I poke my head out and shout up the hall, "Hey Jassem! I'll be ready shortly. Felton, would you please give Jassem one of our family albums from the coffee table to go through."

Finally ready after twenty minutes I stand indecisively in the mirror. If I rush up the hall I will appear anxious and I certainly don't want him to think I am desperate. If I am nonchalant he may think I am not really interested. How crazy. Oh forget this. I walk up the hall to greet Jassem and he nervously hands me a single red rose. The anticipating look on his face said it all. I simply melt into gratefulness. We both seem coincidentally still quite insecure about one another.

It is strange riding with Jassem while pretending to be a tour guide and discussing Memphis history. I suggest we eat at Picadilly's, a traditional buffet near Graceland. I assume him to be a fastidious eater due to his customary cuisine. This is neither lunch nor dinner and I certainly do not object. We are simply enjoying one another's company. No surprise he selects baked fish and vegetables for the both of us and seems pleased with the establishment.

From the short time I have interacted with him he appears patient with sharp listening skills. Perhaps this is due in part to the fact Jassem is an instructor. I think to myself how I would enjoy speaking this beautiful Arabic language. He reaches into his inside coat pocket and hands me two pictures of himself, a larger full-length and a smaller head-shot. On the larger one he is wearing clothing similar to an oversized t-shirt called a dishdasha that men customarily wear in the Middle East. In the smaller picture he is wearing a scarf also customary called kaffiyeh. The rope holding the kaffiyeh is an agal.

His father's name is Ahmed Jassem Al-Hashash. In the Arab culture, switching the middle and first name is how names remain in the family for generation after generation. Al-Hashash is a name dating back literally hundreds of years. Jassem intensely wants me to know who he is, a very proud Kuwaiti. As Rajean explained, Kuwait is a wealthy, oil-rich Muslim country ruled by a king. Jassem is unarguably a fine officer.

After eating I want Jassem to meet a dear friend, Vanessa, before we head to the movies. I telephoned her earlier to make sure she would be at home. Prior to being bused to east Memphis I attended Southside High School around the corner from Vanessa. It is one of the most popular schools in the city. All of their athletic teams, the band, and the high-stepping majorettes are successful competitors.

Vanessa and I bounce thoughts of life off one another either while sipping tea at the International House of Pancakes on Union Avenue, which turned into a regular hangout of ours, or during our ridiculously long neighborhood walks. She refers to me as "little buddy." We get together to either color or cut our hair.

We drive up to Vanessa's home and she is sitting on her front porch step huddled in an oversized coat, smoking a cigarette and offering a large welcoming smile. Her mom walks to the front door to see who we are and waves. Their home is deep in a neighborhood and not like Eloise Street off a main busy boulevard – much quieter. On sizzling summer nights all the magnolia and sycamore trees provide the absolute best cool place to sit and do nothing.

"Hey Vanessa."

"What's up buddy?"

"Vanessa, I want you to meet Jassem."

"So you are the infamous one."

"Excuse me?" he said smiling.

"No. You are the one Pam's been talking about so much every day."

We all laugh. The aroma of a chocolate cake baking in the oven had settled in the warm living room. As I suspected, he and Vanessa have no problems comfortably conversing. She discreetly begins to give way to inquisitive questions about Kuwait, and Jassem – being ever so proud of Kuwait – willingly shares. If she hadn't scrutinized him I would have thought something was wrong with her. Vanessa has a natural way with people. Most are drawn to her and open up rather easily.

The movie takes a back seat again but neither one of us is particularly bothered. During the course of Vanessa figuring Jassem out he suggests later we go to 2001 with a couple of his friends. Will this become our unofficial hangout? Vanessa and I both have a fear of heights but I persuade her that the aerial view of Memphis at night is certainly worth seeing. She gives in and we will return around seven-thirty to pick her up.

"Jassem, it's almost five-thirty now. Are you really going to drive all the way back to Millington and then here again? That's an awful lot of driving."

He smiles and says not to worry.

I anxiously open the car door as soon as Jassem pulls up the driveway so that he can leave quickly. He takes my hand and shakes his head. Jassem turns the engine off and slowly walks over and opens my door. Walking up the steps, he unhurriedly counts them.

"One! Two! Three!"

He kisses my hand and sarcastically says, "Now I will drive like a madman."

He dashes down the steps, races to his car, and blows me a kiss.

Momma is in the kitchen preparing Sunday's dinner and all my sisters are gathered in the dining area. Daddy is relaxing on the couch listening to the radio. I tell Momma Jassem and I were at Vanessa's and he is returning in a couple of hours and we are all going out. She too thinks why would he drive to Millington then immediately turn around and come back.

While we are hanging out in the dining area, Mrs. Winifred taps on the back door. As soon as she enters the room, comical sarcastic comments spew. Stephanie especially favors Mrs. Winifred because she is a jovial lady. I want to leave and prepare for the night but Stephanie of course informed her of the new foreigner in my life.

"Well Ms. Pam. These Eloise scoundrels too much for you too! Huh?"

"Mrs. Winifred, he found me."

"Pam. I like that. He found me. Shucks!"

As laughing fills the room I head back to the bedroom.

Mrs. Winifred and the others are in the dining room when Jassem arrives. It appears his hair is still wet from showering and he is indeed a handsome Kuwaiti. The scent of his expensive cologne overpowers any aroma in the house. I am rummaging in the closet for a scarf to go with my coat and Daddy walks up.

"Good evening, Mr. Williams."

"Good evening. Young man, will you move your car so I can get out please?"

"Yes sir. I will move it right now."

I gathered a coat and scarf and we walked out together.

"Pam. Your father is strict and he doesn't like me. A very strict man!"

"He's not strict. He doesn't know you."

Jassem's two companions are the same friends that were with him the night we met. Latif is wearing a nice leather bomber jacket and is smoking outside the car. Nadel is in the back seat. Yes, they are Kuwaitis – dark and handsome.

The drive to Vanessa's is peculiarly quiet. I can't seem to muster up any small talk. Latif speaks to Jassem in Arabic and he chuckles. Whatever is said prompts him to hold my hand then ask is everything okay.

Vanessa is waiting at the door and waves out as we approach the porch. She is the one with style – hair, boots and all. Jassem introduces Latif and Nadcl as she enters the back seat. Did she have this moment rehearsed? She begins with a litany of questions and his friends eagerly answer, especially Latif.

We dance and enjoy our evening at 2001. Vanessa forgets about her fear of heights and Jassem uses a cocktail napkin to teach me how to write my name and simple words in Arabic. The night ends at one o'clock.

Friends

Daddy opens the front windows to begin airing our home out with the April morning freshness. Everyone is awake and falling into their Saturday ritual of responsibilities. Momma told us earlier in the week we are waxing our wood floors today. We remove the area rug, sweep, and layer the living room, dining room, and hall with paste wax. After the paste hardens, Stephanie and I take turns using the electric buffer. This is the fun portion of cleaning – seeing the floors transform into a slippery immaculate shine.

When Timothy and Marcus were kids they would slide up and down the hall pretending to ski, of course, when Daddy and Momma were away. Marcus was clowning around and slid so hard he crashed into the gas wall heater placing a permanent indention at the bottom near the controls. Daddy was livid. He threatened Timothy and Marcus with dire consequences if either one attempted sliding in the house again.

Jassem, a few of his friends, and I are going to the zoo today. I want to relax but anytime Jassem and I plan to go anywhere I become anxious.

Jassem, Latif, Tawaab, Kayr, and I arrive at the Memphis

Zoo around 11:30. They all seem quite bored with the zoo and the only highlight is the camels. They begin laughing, pointing sarcastically and speaking in Arabic. Jassem too! They were accustomed to better-bred camels. Jassem tells me these are the most pitiful looking camels alive and will not tell me what else they are saying. I am speechless.

On the weekends we have spent all our time together and this one is no different. After the zoo, we stop by a fast food eatery for lunch and it is crowded. After Jassem orders our food I hear a worker ask another if I am black. I look at her and don't utter a sound. I am slightly insulted. Does it matter if I am whatever? Our culture is so permeated with elements of racism it is simply unavoidable at times. I am thankful to God for Jassem and meeting his friends. They are all Kuwaitis and they don't distinguish one another by skin color. What a profound lesson in life to learn. There is a world outside of mine that doesn't operate on this racial premise.

Jassem and I go back to the BOQ. He has an important exam next week and needs to study. He feels comfortable and prefers me with him when he is studying on the weekends. I frankly don't see how he does this. I turn the television down low and sometimes read.

The phone rings and it is Tawaab. He has some additional materials for Jassem to study and wants him to come by and pick them up. Jassem has been studying for three hours and a break is nice right about now. Tawaab, who's married, lives off base in an apartment really close by.

We arrive at Tawaab's and the unfamiliar aroma of Arabic food is enough to have anyone salivating. There are five guys sitting on the floor in a circle around a white tablecloth, bowls, and rice. The center has something similar to a potholder and the main course must be in the kitchen. I know three of the five young men and Jassem introduces me to the others. Tawaab's apartment is a typical bachelor pad – nothing extra, only the basics. Tawaab invites us to remain and eat but I adamantly refuse. I feel uncomfortable and do not want to spoil the male-dominated ambiance.

Tawaab and Jassem go into the back room and I head into the kitchen to see what the host is preparing. One of the guests comes into the kitchen while the others continue talking.

"Hello."

"Hi. Tawaab must be an excellent cook. This food smells delicious," I said.

"You Americans think you have it made in the shade don't you?"

"Excuse me?"

"I said you Americans think you are so special and have it made as you would say."

"I don't know what you mean or what you are talking about."

I smile and nervously attempt to leave the kitchen but he turns to me and is waiting for a response. I am uncomfortable. Jassem steps in the kitchen and immediately notices something is out of sorts. He speaks to the young man in Arabic and the next thing I know they are speaking sharply to each other. Everyone rushes into the kitchen and Tawaab apologizes to me. As the young man sits down, the others seem as though they are chastising him. Again, I hone in on those facial expressions and hand gestures. Jassem takes my hand along with the papers and we hurriedly leave.

"Pam, please ignore anything he said. That one is crazy. He's touched in the head."

Tawaab runs down behind us and apologizes profusely.

"Pam, I am very sorry this happened to you. Please do not take him to heart. His heart is confused and dark. Muslims are good people. I am so sorry."

"Thank you, Tawaab. I am okay and I know Muslims are good people."

"Thank you, Pam."

Tawaab is deeply offended by his guest's actions toward me and sincerely wants me to know. Jassem asks me to get in the car while he and Tawaab talk. They hug and we leave.

"Are you okay?"

"Sure. I am fine. Jassem, people are the same all over the world I guess. Some good and otherwise."

"This is true."

My new Arab friends I presupposed to be flawless are human with frailties.

The Legitimacy of Variation

I am beyond astonishment when Jassem asks to join me for evening worship service. I thought as Muslims they were forbidden to enter a church. I am intrigued by knowing his interest in every facet of my life especially now religion. I've spoken about church often enough I guess to prove to him how proud I too am of the way we worship – what shameless competitiveness. This will be one evening I'll cherish and hopefully an introduction for many more.

Aunt Bell is expecting me to ride with her so I mustn't forget to let her know there is a change in plans. No need to offer her a ride. It is an unwritten rule my independent grandmother drives herself everywhere and almost an insult to suggest anything else.

She too is extremely surprised to know Jassem is going with me to evening worship, and hopes maybe one day he would believe in Jesus Christ and be added to the Church. I shake my head in disagreement and reassure Aunt Bell he loves his own religion. I bid her good-bye and she watches as I walk down her steep rock-filled drive and open the driveway gate.

We arrive at the building on time and he is intrigued by the warmness of the church members. He is in his element behaving as a foreigner. We locate an area to sit directly below the edge of the balcony. Aunt Bell enters and sits in her usual pew. I turn around and wave. Jassem walks over and shakes her hand. Aunt Bell smiles modestly. I suspect he could do no wrong in her eyes.

Seeing Christian men and women worshiping together in a religious assembly must be a historical event for him. Muslim men and women pray and worship separately. Momma clearly remembers when she was younger, men and women did sit separately in the Church of Christ – women on the left and men on the right. And, women traditionally covered their heads always with hats, especially in the South.

Daddy does not believe women should wear pants to worship and he never purchased pants for his daughters. Momma bought my first pair of bell-bottom pants when I was in junior high school. To this day I am more comfortable in dresses. Momma says several customs subtly changed with time.

The song leader steps to the podium and leads the congregation in the hymn: "I am the vine and ye are the branches. I am the vine, be faithful and true. Ask what ye will, your prayers shall be answered. The Father loved me, so I have loved you…"

Jassem whispers, "Doesn't your church have a piano?"

"Piano! We don't have pianos in worship. Sweetheart, you read the wrong book," I reply facetiously.

"What book?"

"Jassem, never mind. Shh!"

The Churches of Christ do not use musical instruments to accompany our singing. The early Christians and even the synagogues did not use instruments and we are following that example. Modern historians agree the music of the early church was without a doubt, vocal. We believe no authority has been given to use musical instruments in the most Holy place to worship the One True Living God. We believe this to be sectarian – the Holy scriptures do not teach thus, there is no commandment given and it goes beyond what the scriptures allow. Instead, we use our natural God-given instrument – the voice, which is a cappella. The use of instrumental music in the church began several centuries later, after a.d. 300.

Jassem is reading the bulletin and as Brother Lambert begins his sermon, he asks another question.

"Is he Reverend Lambert?"

"No. I mean yes. Jassem, we don't call our ministers reverends and yes he is Brother Lambert, our minister."

He smiles and attentively listens.

The Church of Christ objects to ministers being called "Reverend" or "Pastor." In New Testament times, the word "Pastor" was a synonym for Elder. It was first used by Paul in Acts 20:17: And from Miletus he sent to Ephesus, and called the elders of the church. Peter was an elder. 1 Peter 5:1-2: The elders which are among you I exhort, who am also an elder, and a witness of the sufferings of Christ, and also a partaker of the glory that shall be revealed: Feed the flock of God which is among you, taking the oversight thereof, not by constraint, but willingly; not for filthy lucre, but of a ready mind. Biblically, the shepherds of the flock are the bishops or elders, not the preacher. There was always more than one single pastor in any congregation. Some preachers are also Pastors and Elders – most are not.

The use of the word Reverend is a religious title forbidden by Christ himself in Matthew 23:8-12: But be not ye called Rabbi: for one is your Master, even Christ; and all ye are brethren. And call no man your father upon the earth: for one is your Father, which is in heaven. Neither be ye called masters: for one is your Master, even Christ. But he that is greatest among you shall be your servant. And whosoever shall exalt himself shall be abased; and he that shall humble himself shall be exalted.

The word Reverend is used only once in the bible in which something is honored in reverence, Psalms 111:9: He sent redemption unto his people: he hath commanded his covenant for ever: holy and reverend is his name. Again, there is no commandment given and it is improper.

Within the last several years many Churches of Christ now have Bishops. 1 Timothy 3:1-3: This is a true saying, if a man desire the office of a bishop, he desireth a good work. A bishop then must be blameless, the husband of one wife, vigilant, sober, of good behavior, given to hospitality, apt to teach. Not given to wine, no striker, not greedy of filthy lucre; but patient, not a brawler, not covetous.

Jassem, within a few minutes of sharing this experience with me, is learning basic practices and beliefs of the Churches of Christ. I assumed he knew most but it is an error on my part to think he did. After all I am a Christian and he is a Muslim.

Brother Lambert is well into the sermon and Jassem softly asks, "Pam. Do you believe what he says?"

"Of course I do."

"These are lies, Pam. You must not believe this man."

"What?"

"This man lies to his people. The only way to heaven, and Jesus is God's son."

Jassem folds his arms and covers his mouth with a frozen, perplexed expression. I bow my head in disgust. How dare he call Brother Lambert a liar! Disagree but don't speak these horrible things. What does he think is a lie? Everything Brother Lambert stated I believe. This is insane. How can Jassem speak so harshly?

I turn to him and my eyes reveal an aggrieved spirit. He realizes his words caused me grief and he puts his arm around me with a "dismissive" sigh, determined to listen. I slightly move my shoulder away from him and he pulls me closer. Always without fail Jassem safeguarded our relationship with immediate communications to avoid misunderstandings – he loathed friction. I am too disturbed and unable to concentrate on the preaching. I want to cry. Instead, I sit staring at Brother Lambert. God help me speak civilly to Jassem when we leave here. I love him but he can't ever speak about the Church or Brother Lambert in this manner to me again, ever. Is this the end for us?

Think, Pam, think. He is reacting to something he does not understand or believe. If I were in a mosque would I respond as he did? I think not – certainly not to the point of outwardly condemning. Oh well, tonight is not turning out the way I planned.

Brother Lambert ends his sermon and states the Church of Christ plan of salvation as he always does.

"Acts 4:12: Neither is there salvation in any other: for there is none other name under heaven given among men, whereby we must be saved. To become a member of the Lord's church you must first, hear. Romans 10:17: So then faith cometh by hearing, and hearing by the word of God. Believe. John 3:16: For God so loved the world, that he gave his only begotten Son, that whosoever believeth in him should not perish, but have everlasting life. Repent. Luke 13:3: I tell you, Nay; but, except ye repent, ye shall all likewise perish. Confess. Matthew 10:32: Whosoever therefore shall confess me before men, him will I confess also before my Father which is in heaven.

And last be baptized for the remission of sins. Acts 2:38: Then Peter said unto them, 'Repent, and be baptized every one of you in the Name of Jesus Christ for the remission of sins and ye shall receive the gift of the Holy Ghost. And after you rise from the watery grave, you shall rise as a new creature."

The song leader stood up and the congregation followed, singing an invitational hymn, "All things are ready come to the feast. Come for the table now is spread. Ye famishing, ye weary, come and thou shall be richly fed..."

A young man walks to the front and sits down in one of the benches. An elder joins him with a pen and pad to record his name and the reason for him responding. After the last chorus, the song leader motions the congregation to be seated. The elder speaks with Brother Lambert and afterwards announces the young man desires to be baptized. Brother Lambert walks over and takes his hand.

"Theophilus Miller, do you believe Jesus Christ is the Son of God?"

"Yes."

"That he died and rose on the third day?"

"Yes."

"You will now be baptized for the remission of your sins and you will receive the gift of the Holy Ghost. You will now be added to the Church and rise as a new creature." Brother Lambert nods and two men walk over and guide him to the area behind the pulpit to prepare for baptism.

"Pam. What is going on?"

I do not answer Jassem.

"Pam."

I look at him with a disagreeable smirk and turn my head. Jassem again puts his arm around me and continues to study every aspect of service.

"The young man confessed he believes Jesus is the Son of God and now he is going to be baptized. You'll see."

Jesus was baptized. He considered baptism significant enough to walk 60 to 70 miles from Nazareth to be baptized by John in the Jordan River. Baptism is symbolic to the burial and resurrection of Jesus Christ and is an outward confession of belief. The New Testament teaches complete immersion in water is baptism and is an act which is essential to salvation. It washes away sin and places us into the church. (Matthew 3:13-17: Then cometh Jesus from Galilee to Jordan unto John, to be baptized of him. But John forbad him, saying, I have need to be baptized of thee, and comest thou to me? And Jesus answering said unto him, Suffer it to be so now: for thus it becometh us to fulfill all righteousness. Then he suffered him. And Jesus, when he was baptized, went up straightway out of the water: and, lo, the heavens were opened unto him, and he saw the Spirit of God descending like a dove, and lighting upon him: And lo a voice from heaven, saying, This is my beloved Son, in whom I am well pleased.)

Jassem is awestruck as he observes the baptism and the remainder of service. While I am still fuming, his demeanor of challenge and disbelief is now that of a respectful observer. Perhaps this genuine evening compelled a better side of him.

Service ends and we walk Aunt Bell to her car. I struggle with whether or not to ride back with Jassem. He attempts time after time to resume some sort of conversation. I cannot.

Sadly, as a little girl when I was deeply bothered or angry, I could refrain from uttering one word for days. My parents became so accustomed to this repeated idiosyncratic behavior I overheard Momma tell Daddy once I usually break the silence in two to three days.

A few blocks away from home Jassem makes a U-turn. I simply am not concerned with what he is planning. I sit nonchalantly. We drive back in the direction towards church. Initially, I think we are going back to the building for some odd reason but instead, he drives past it. This is interesting. He doesn't know where he is going. Or does he? We drive through Beale Street and he is heading for Tom Lee Park. We visited this park on our first date. He parks the car and walks around, opens my door, and squats.

"Pam. Now let's talk."

"I don't feel like talking. Take me home."

"No, Pam. You are very angry with me and this is not good at all. I am sorry I offended you. Please forgive me."

I say nothing. My heart is breaking seeing Jassem this way and I can't gather my thoughts. He gets back in the car and as he turns the key I take his hand.

"Jassem, please forgive me for being so rude to you. I didn't mean it. I was only hurt."

"Pam, you are my life. You cannot imagine how much I love you. Swear to me we will always talk trouble out. Swear!"

"You know I don't swear but I can promise you."

Christians do not swear. James 5:12: But above all things, my brethren, swear not, neither by heaven, neither by the earth, neither by any other oath: but let your yea be yea; and your nay, nay; lest ye fall into condemnation.

We walk to the edge of the park and look at the reflections on the Mississippi River. Jassem explains Muslims believe Jesus was a great prophet who performed miracles and healing but they do not believe he is the Son of God. Muslims believe the Prophet Muhammad (peace be upon him) is the true prophet of God and a direct descendant. When Brother Lambert stated Jesus is the Son of God, it angered Jassem.

Muslims respect and hold Jesus in high honor. They consider him to be one of God's greatest messengers to mankind and he was born to the virgin Mary. When the angels said (Qu'ran 3:45-47), "O Mary, God gives you good news of a word from Him (GOD), whose name is the Messiah Jesus, son of Mary, revered in this world and the Hereafter, and one of those brought near (to God). He will speak to the people from his cradle and as a man, and he is of the righteous." She said, "My Lord, how can I have a child when no mortal has touched me?" He said, "so (it will be). God creates what He wills. If He decrees a thing, He says to it only, Be!" and it is.

Muslims believe Jesus was not crucified. Qu'ran 4:157: It was the plan of Jesus' enemies to crucify him, but God saved him and raised him up to Him. And the likeness of Jesus was put over another man. Jesus' enemies took this man and crucified him, thinking that he was Jesus. They said, "We killed the Messiah Jesus, son of Mary, the messenger of God," They did not kill him, nor did they crucify him, but the likeness of him was put on another man (and they killed that man).

An Imam is similar to our minister or spiritual leader if you will. The Imam is the one who leads the prayer during Islamic gatherings. In smaller communities an Imam could be the community leader.

Muslims observe five formal prayers each day. The timing of these prayers is spaced fairly evenly throughout the day, so that one is constantly reminded of God and given opportunities to seek His guidance and forgiveness. Muslims observe the formal prayers at the following times:

Fajr (pre-dawn): This prayer starts off the day with the remembrance of God; it is performed before sunrise.

Dhuhr (noon): After the day's work has begun, one breaks shortly after noon to again remember God and seek His guidance.

'Asr (afternoon): In the late afternoon, people are usually busy wrapping up the day's work, getting kids home from school, etc. It is an important time to take a few minutes to remember God and the greater meaning of our lives.

Maghrib (sunset): Just after the sun goes down, Muslims remember God again as the day begins to come to a close.

'Isha (evening): Before retiring for the night, Muslims again take time to remember God's presence, guidance, mercy and forgiveness.

In Muslim communities people are reminded of the daily prayer times through the calling of the adhan – the Islamic call to prayer.

I explain the Bible consists of two testaments or covenants (solemn declarations) – the Old and New Testament. The Old Testament consists of the creation, issues of humanity, the fall of man, and more importantly, the prophecies of Christ. The New Testament tells of the fulfillment of the prophecies from the Old Testament and how to live your life as a Christian. Thus, we consider ourselves saved and live by the New Covenant, not the Old.

This is a crystallizing moment for Jassem and me. Out of sheer necessity we must be patient and understanding with one another's religion that we hold so dearly to our hearts – even if we vehemently disagree.

What I presupposed to be one of the most dreadful evenings for us and perhaps an end to our relationship evolved into a deeper commitment and love for each other.

Tonight is a night of beliefs – believing in one another and more importantly, in our faiths.

Thank you God!

Grandmother's Death

Momma's stepmother, "Big Momma," has cancer and she is not expected to live through the weekend. This is Momma's father's second wife. Big Momma had not been the kindest parent to them – plain evil at times from what I heard. Despite this character flaw, Momma insists on doing right by her. Yes, she cared for them and consequently she and Uncle Joseph did not have to spend their youth in an orphanage when their father abandoned them.

She lives in north Memphis, and many parts of that area have huge multi-level homes with basements and attics. Too many monster movies caused me to dislike homes with what seemed to have several nooks and crannies. She resides on a one-way street and the home is large and on an incline with a garage in the rear. She conducted business from her home as a beautician and it held the scent of hair chemicals like that of a beauty salon.

Momma is over there along with her stepsister everyday, caring and comforting. She arrives there in the morning and returns home in the afternoon to prepare for her evening job. She is starting to look tired. I want to help but Momma insists we stay away. Her generation and older is adamantly against children visiting people with cancer. Some of those deeply rooted idiosyncratic ideologies of the South remain unchanged.

Big Momma has taken a turn for the worse. The minister and family are called to come immediately. Marcus telephones me to say he is going over and offers to drive us. Marcus is a jokester at heart but when it came to matters such as this, he is quite the solemn one.

Momma is standing in the door when we arrive and is relieved to see us. We take turns going in so not to disturb Big Momma during this fleeing of life. As I walk towards her bed, the very tall large-framed woman known as "Big Momma" is now reduced to a small, weak, frail human silhouette of death. I softly stroke her arms and hold her hand while kissing her forehead. She opens her eyes and smiles at me. She enjoys the soap operas, and the television volume is low to a whisper – this is her request. She passes away later this evening.

Monday, April 3, 1978

Because her death was imminent funeral arrangements were preplanned. The service is scheduled for Friday at six o'clock at a local Baptist church where she has been a member for decades.

I telephone Jassem and tell him the news and he offers to go with me to the services. Through the remainder of the week, Momma's long list of friends visit bringing dishes of food and desserts. She seems to be taking it well. Uncle Joseph in California is not coming.

Friday

We are all in preparation to leave and my sisters and I are riding with Jassem. Carolyn is standing watch at the front door for Jassem. Stephanie, Melinda, and I are in the dining room nibbling on one of the pound cakes delivered this week. This will be the second time in my life visiting a Baptist church. Because we sing a cappella in the Church of Christ, hearing an organ with people singing marks a major milestone for all of us.

"Here he is. Here is Jassem."

"I hope those people at Big Momma's church don't start all that shouting and stuff," Stephanie remarks.

"I doubt it. This is a funeral. Not a regular service." I reply.

"Well, Pam, you never know," Stephanie insists.

Before Jassem can make it to the front porch steps, we all walk out. Other than me providing directions to Jassem, there is complete silence in the car the entire time. As we drive into the parking lot, the funeral attendants are busy escorting people into the building and handing out obituaries while others start lining the family up in the appropriate relationship order for seating. We discreetly make our way to the end of the line, then we are abruptly stopped and directed to go closer to the front. I knew if for any reason this funeral required an immediate exit, sitting in the rear made it easier. It's too late now.

I am accustomed to male ushers and seeing the female ushers in white uniforms and gloves is perplexing. They are standing in all the aisles near the family section closely observing everyone. Their roles are to accommodate the family, especially if someone becomes emotionally distressed. Jassem smiles at me from time to time and holds my hand.

After the eulogy, the minister states Big Momma is now in heaven looking down on us.

It is time to view Big Momma's body. As the ushers approach our row, Jassem slightly nudges me with his arm. His face is red-flushed and he is shaking his head. By then we have stood up and walked towards the casket. Jassem barely looks and does not stop. As we head down the aisle I veer to the right to walk outside. Jassem is mumbling to himself and something is wrong.

"Pam, don't ever do that to me again," he says in an upset voice.

"What! What is wrong with you? What are you talking about?"

"Let's go."

We hurry to the car and he opens my door, still looking at me, angrily shaking his head. He removes his jacket while walking to the other side. Jassem is upset and I am completely disconcerted.

"Why didn't you tell me?"

"Tell you what?"

"I did not know we were going to see your grandmother's body. Let's go. I will take you home."

"Wait. I need to tell my sisters I am leaving so they can ride back with someone else."

I find Marcus and tell him we are leaving and to give my sisters a ride back. When I sit in the car the air is at its highest level and Jassem has taken his glasses off, placing them on the dashboard while something short of panting.

"Jassem, I am sorry. You know I would not have asked you to be here if this funeral caused you to be this uncomfortable or upset you."

This is the first time it appeared Jassem is truly upset with me and it does not feel good. Too many customs! Who could know them all? Minutes pass and still not a word. Turning onto Eloise Street, I begin gathering my purse and the folded obituaries while removing the seat belt. He takes my hand and kisses it. Immediately I open the door as he turns the car off.

"Wait, Pam!"

"Jassem, you know in my heart I would not do anything to offend you or what you believe. I should have taken more time and explained how we conduct funerals."

"Pam, it is my responsibility to share with you the ways of Islam and I should have asked about yours."

"Oh well. Jassem I guess I know now what to do if someone else dies."

He smiles and nodded in agreement.

"I love you, Pam."

"I love you more. I'll call you later. Goodnight."

Jassem was accepting of most customs regarding the funeral. However, seeing our grandmother's deceased body was the major offense.

When the death of a Muslim occurs the body is washed, shrouded, and buried immediately, unlike Christians, who embalm and delay burials for various reasons. A shroud is a winding cloth used to wrap a body for burial – usually white cotton.

Following the coffin is recommended for men only. Women are forbidden in these types of crowds for their own protection so as to avoid any potential incident and close contact.

The actual burying of the dead is quite different from Christians. From the time of the Prophet until today, it is a Muslim custom to place the dead body in the grave on its right side with the face of the dead person towards the Qiblah – the direction of the sacred shrine of the Ka'bah in Mecca.

A Rose

Yesterday marked six months since we first met but my heart has always known Jassem.

The summer sound and smell of fresh rhythmic raindrops softly splattering against the upstairs balcony of the Bachelor Officers Quarters awakens me. It is nine o'clock in the morning and this is the second time I decided to spend the night with Jassem. The pressure of completely loving him and respecting my parents' household is emotionally intense – I had an occasion to exude anger – this is another one of those times. As I awaken, Jassem is robed and toweling his wet hair. He had been up for some time watching the rain and allowing me to sleep undisturbed. He offers me some of his orange juice and as I refuse, he quickly senses my agitation and suggests we go to breakfast and talk, but I decline this as well. I want to go home.

As we leave the base area restaurants line the boulevard and he purposely drives slowly towards the interstate asking again if I changed my mind and wanted something to eat. He takes my hand and holds it to his chest. I can no longer restrain my frustration.

"Jassem, the entire family now knows I spent the night with you again!"

"I know, Pam. I am very sorry!"

"Sorry! What in heaven's name are you sorry for? It's not your family."

"I don't like to see you this way and I can tell you are quite upset. Do you regret staying with me?"

"Jassem. It's nothing. Don't worry about it. No, I don't regret anything and I mean anything. It is facing my parents, especially Daddy. It's like our secret is out or something. I feel awful."

Jassem turns my chin towards him, smiling, and says, "Pam, everything is going to be fine. Do you love me?"

"Why are you asking me this now? You know I do."

"Let's get married."

"What!"

"Marry me."

"Jassem pull over. Now!"

He quickly drives the car onto the emergency lane and turns towards me with his arms folded, smiling mischievously.

"And!" I asked.

"Pam. Let's get married?"

"Are you asking me to marry you?"

Jassem smiles.

"Yes, I will marry you."

Jassem removes his glasses and kisses me.

"Pam we are going to be fine. I want to be with you all the time and you want to be with me. This is what we must do."

"Jassem, I am oh so afraid to be this happy. It's weird."

"I want you to remain happy and only think of good things in the future. Pam. I need to go home soon to take care of some matters. I will tell you about them later."

"You are going back to Kuwait. When? For how long and what matters?"

"Didn't you hear me say I will tell you later, Pam? You worry too much. Enjoy this moment."

"Wow! We are getting married. Then you tell me you are going home. Any more surprises? I can only take so much. Oh Mr. Al-Hashash, so you are going to be my husband?"

"And Pam, you are going to be my wife."

The idea of us spending the rest of our lives together is simply unbelievable. Jassem is too analytical not to have given this some serious time and forethought. I am confident he will tell me what he needs to take care of in Kuwait. As we merge back onto the interstate, the downpour ceases and a beautiful rainbow appears across the sky.

When he reaches our drive I notice both of the cars in the carport, which means Momma and Daddy are both home. He starts to open the door and I stop him.

"No."

"Please, I want to go in with you or at least let me walk you to the door."

"No."

"I think I need to go in with you."

"Jassem. I don't think it is a good time right now. I'll call you later. Okay!"

"I just asked you to marry me."

"I know, sweetheart, and I love you to death but this is

extremely serious. Please let's wait before we say anything to them. Please."

"Pam, my better opinion tells me I should walk in with you."

"I'll call you later, Jassem. Bye."

"I love you, Pam."

"And I love you more."

Jassem is protective of me even if it pertains to my parents. He kisses my hand as I leave the car and watches me walk up the back steps to the side door, waving for him to leave.

The door is open and as I enter, Daddy is in the kitchen wiping down the stove. I speak to him and he says nothing – this is completely out of character. This is not good. Not good at all.

I heard Momma on the telephone spraying starch while ironing in the front room. I gather clean clothes for bathing. I walk up the hall and speak to Momma. She nods and continued to talk.

As I start up the hall, Daddy goes into their bedroom and calls me in. My heart is palpitating as I slowly walk over to him. He is sitting on the edge of the bed and asks me to close the door.

"Pam, God created beautiful roses. They brighten the world and make people happy. They are most beautiful when you watch and admire them. When a rose is touched, the petals begin to fall off and it starts to lose its beauty. Pretty soon all the petals are gone and the rose is no more."

How desperately I want to tell Daddy about Jassem's proposal of marriage but I do not have the courage.

Instead, I stand in utter stillness listening and looking directly at him as one tear flows down my cheek.

Daddy is undeniably hurt and his face is transparent with disappointment.

"You can go now."

It is difficult for young couples to be in love and not be physically attracted to one another – it's only natural. However natural it may be, it is always best to marry and avoid the potential emotional and physical uncertainties of doing otherwise.

Muslim men can only marry non-Muslim women who are "People of the Book" – chaste Christians and Jews. In Islam, the People of the Book (Arabic – Ahl al-Kitab) are non-Muslim people who according to the Qur'an received scriptures that were revealed to them by God before the time of the Prophet Muhammad (peace be upon him) – especially Christians and Jews. Also, the woman must be practicing her religion at the time of marriage.

Both Islam and Christianity teach to abstain from any sexual activity until marriage and uphold chastity. This is a commandment from both the Qur'an and the Bible.

Qu'ran 17:32 (Al-Isra): And come not near to the unlawful sexual intercourse, Verily it is a transgression of Allah's limits, and an evil way.

2 Timothy 2:22: Flee also youthful lusts: but follow righteousness, faith, charity, peace, with them that call on the Lord out of a pure heart.

The Secret

Professor Natalie Gregory's Communications class is one never taken for granted, not to mention always full to capacity. A small-framed black woman, her perfectly shaped afro and large ethnic earrings highlight her attire. Her eloquent enunciation flows melodiously as she sharply speaks through the last syllable of each word.

Most students are unduly intimidated by this subdued arrogance and they simply listen in hopes of taking quantifiable notes. Whenever a courageous student comments in error, she is merciless in correcting them. However eccentric her style and imperialistic demeanor, she is the professor we all will remember and refer to many years from now. She teaches us confidence, speech and presentation that permeate our young adult minds.

If Professor Gregory stops, peers over her dark green specs, and plays with her fingers, dialogue with a victim ensues. Seemingly, for no apparent reason other than her wanting to do so, a student would be singled out. I maintain a look of "see I am interested, please don't say anything to me" and remarkably it has worked effectively – I thought – except for this evening.

With her back towards me, I quickly turn around

to check the time. She perhaps purposely had the classroom arranged to prevent us from monitoring the time on the oversized clock on the back wall. Knowing her, this room set-up easily traps any anxious victim into embarrassment.

I must be mad to think these thoughts or be overly excited to see Jassem. He is never late picking me up so there really is no need for me to worry. Before I realize what I have done, a soft sigh escapes. The professor immediately stops and slowly turns facing the class. Dear God! It is too late. A young lady sitting to the right of me with a damning stare sifts me out. My arched rolling eye worsens as I stare back at this classroom coward. Well the verdict is locked. In a surprisingly pleasant voice, Professor Gregory looks directly at me.

"Whoever is tired or b-o-o-o-red this evening is certainly free by all means to leave my class!"

I smile pleasantly and look down in the book. The professor sits on the edge of her desk and continues lecturing until the bell sounds.

I race up the wide flight of stairs through the double doors and Jassem is there sitting on the car smiling as I walk up. He hugs me for dear life.

"I should go to class more often. I love this type of greeting."

He smiles and said nothing but only looks at me and starts driving towards downtown as opposed to taking me home. We are headed to our favorite spot, Tom Lee Park.

"Would you get me a tissue out of the glove box?"

I open the glove compartment and a small jewelry box falls out.

"I hope you like it."

"This is mine."

He smiles as I open the box. Inside is a gold ring with two hearts and diamonds inside each heart.

"It isn't an engagement ring, just a little something special I wanted you to have."

"Jassem, it is beautiful. Thank you."

He places the ring on my finger and we kiss.

Jassem tells me he is going back to Kuwait in a week to obtain permission for us to get married. Being a Kuwaiti officer he is obligated to his country first and because I am neither a citizen nor Muslim it complicates matters. He attempts earnestly to explain a few details but it offers no clear reasoning as far as I am concerned. The simplicities of the only culture I've known seem rather minuscule in comparison to his.

Complications continue to mire the evening.

"Pam, do you truly believe I love you?"

"Of course. You know I do!"

"I never dreamed I would ever meet someone like you. You have changed my life forever. Our falling in love has changed many things. No, it has changed everything. Pam, I need to tell you something extremely important."

Jassem has a sober look about him.

"Jassem, come on with whatever it is you need to tell me because you're scaring me a little. Tell me what?"

"I am engaged to marry my cousin back in Kuwait."

"What did you just say? Is this some type of cruel joke? It isn't funny!"

"It's true, Pam. Believe me. I am not joking."

"No! No! What! You tell me this now after all these

months. What is this ring for? What were you thinking, Jassem? Evidently you were only thinking of yourself. Engaged! How can you ask me to marry you when you are engaged to someone else? Your cousin! What is wrong with you? What do you expect me to say? Dear God! Take me home. Take me home now and take this ring. What is wrong with you?"

I take the ring off and throw it at him.

"Pam! Pam! Listen to me! Please listen carefully. I love you and I did not expect to meet you and fall in love. It changed everything. I tell you everything. How can I love anyone after loving you? How can I marry anyone after loving you? I can't. This is why I want to marry you! I want to be with you, Pam. I had to tell you the truth because I do love you. You are my life."

"I am your life. Oh no! You betrayed me! You betrayed me! You make me sick! For the last time, I said take me home! Now! Now, Jassem!"

"Pam, please listen to me. This matter is not a simple one and I must go home to deal with it. I had to tell you. You must believe me."

"I am sick and tired of hearing about Kuwait rules and what is not simple! Tired!"

I begin crying uncontrollably and ask him again to take me home immediately. He fumbles and picks the ring off the car floor. He tries to hold my hand but I take my fist and hit him in the chest. He sits back and takes a deep breath. We go back and forth about taking me home and it almost erupts into a physical fight. Jassem refuses to take me home and insists I go with him to the base. After twenty minutes or so, I finally succumb and agree to go with him. I begin to get physically ill and feel like vomiting.

Fate would have it that Nuri shows up as we are walking into Jassem's room. Obvious disgust is mirrored on our faces. He begins speaking to Jassem in Arabic and I understand one or two words and that is it. Jassem opens the door and I go inside while they continue talking outside.

Nuri is older and highly respected by Jassem and the others. He studies and remains close to the base and I never hear Jassem mention him going out. The door finally opens and it is Nuri.

"Pam, this man loves you very much. Believe this. Good night!" And he leaves.

Jassem walks in and sits down in the chair at his desk and I am sitting on the edge of the sofa.

"Jassem, what am I supposed to say to you right about now?"

He looks at me and tears stream down his face. Seeing him this way is too much to handle – it hurts at the pit of my heart. Jassem is the love of my life and I don't know how to respond. Dear God, what do I do? He opens his arms and I walk over and hold his head to my chest.

"Jassem, I love you and I don't want to lose you. But our situation scares me. All of these months and not one word! Not a word. Another woman loves you and is expecting you to marry her too! You need to clean this mess up. You belong to me, not this woman. What are you going to say to her when you go back to Kuwait? How in God's name can you not see her? I am weak and sick of talking about it. Jassem, like I said, you need to clean this mess up!"

"Pam you are my life and you don't have any idea what you mean to me. You simply cannot imagine."

"Jassem," I sighed.

Daddy's words of the rose are fresh in my mind. I don't want to leave Jassem especially tonight, but I must. He hesitantly takes me home and tonight I realize I can't live without him.

The School Night Visit

The next day Vanessa calls and asks me to come over. She seems anxious to talk. I will not tell her about Jassem's engagement. Her reaction may make me feel even more devastated than I already am.

When I arrive she offers me tea and we sit on the back porch. Jassem visited her last night and she says he was deeply disturbed. She is nervous sharing this with me.

"Pam, you know I would not lie to you. I'm telling you he came over last night."

"Vanessa, he's only been here a couple of times. How did he know how to get to your house from school?"

"All I can tell you is he stopped by here after he dropped you off. Pam, I don't know what to make out of it except to say Jassem loves you. I mean an awful lot. You know when I opened the door and saw him quite naturally I looked for you. He had dropped you off at school and wanted to talk to me. The entire time he was here he kept looking at his watch to be sure to pick you up on time. His exact words were 'Vanessa, I love Pam so much. She is my life and I don't know what to do.' Pam he was almost in tears. He was pitiful. No I mean pitiful and pouring his heart out about you. Whatever is bothering him is tearing him up inside. And wait, I am not finished. He also said he could never love anyone else after loving you. I asked him what did he mean by that and he looked at me and didn't say anything."

Vanessa points to the couch.

"He sat right there most of the time with his head down, Pam."

"Vanessa, he gave me this ring last night and asked me to marry him two nights ago."

"Two nights ago! And you are just telling me. Okay. I know you. What's wrong?"

"I wanted us to be together when we told you. That's all."

"Congratulations buddy. And of course you said yes?"

"I did. He gave me this beautiful heart ring but it's not an engagement ring."

"I am so happy for you. This is really a nice ring. Is that what was bothering him? Good grief, Pam! I was worried there for a moment. I thought he had some sickness or something. Okay, why are you not jumping up and screaming like the Pam I know. The love of your life has asked you to marry him and you sit here acting like Miss Calm or something. What's up?"

"A little dark cloud I guess. Jassem and I cannot walk into a courthouse and get married. He needs permission or something like that. As an officer of the Kuwait Air Force he is contracted or obligated to his country to abide by certain rules, I think. I am not sure. Anyway, he's going home in a week to get it taken care of."

"Pam! What kind of mess is that? I have never heard of anything like this before in my life. That's bull."

"Jassem has a lot on his mind, Vanessa, and I am guessing he wanted to talk it out with you but decided not to. Remember he is not from here and I am slowly finding out other countries have an entirely different set of rules and laws of the land. How do you suppose I felt when he was explaining all of this to me? Vanessa, I trust him unconditionally and I must believe whatever he is doing or going to do for that matter is going to keep us together. Jassem is going to work this out so I am not going to start worrying. By the way, I have decided until Jassem has all of this figured out let's keep it between us. This isn't a normal situation. First, he is a foreigner from the other side of the world and second he worships differently. Oh let's not forget this means I am going to leave this country."

"Don't worry, buddy. I won't say a word. Wow. I don't want to think about you leaving. Are you ready for that? We know Jassem will do everything and anything to make you safe and happy. Pam, I can cry right now."

"Please don't cry. Jassem will have all these loose ends tied very soon and we can all rest a little easier."

Jassem Leaves for Kuwait

Jassem is going home tomorrow and said he has a pleasant surprise for me today. He provided no hints only to say he will be here around noon. I have been praying to God to please work everything out for us. The road ahead is not going to be an easy one but as long as we are together we will work through this.

He arrives on time and I do not see a package with him.

"Okay, Jassem, where is the surprise?"

"It's coming. I need to use your phone."

Our phone in the hall has a 20-foot-long extension cord to reach every room in the house. I bring the phone to him in the living room and he begins dialing several numbers.

"Don't worry. I charged it to my phone."

Jassem begins speaking in Arabic and whoever is on the other end fills him with elation. He speaks my name twice and then hands the phone to me.

"Talk to my mother."

"Your mom! Why didn't you tell me before now?"

"Talk to her. She's waiting."

"Hello. Hello Mrs. Al-Hashash."

I cannot understand one word she is saying. She is

speaking in Arabic and sparse English. I draw a blank with the Arabic Jassem taught me. Why is it I can only remember how to say yes? Goodness. I hand the phone back to Jassem and he asks me to get Momma.

"Momma! Come here! Please hurry!"

She rushes up the hallway.

"What's wrong?"

"Nothing's wrong. Jassem is talking to his mother and would like for you to talk to her."

"Your mother! This is certainly a surprise. Okay, give me the phone. Hello! Nice to talk to you too!"

Momma undoubtedly has a much more difficult time than I did trying to understand his mother. She hands Jassem back the phone and we both stand gawking as though we understand Arabic. Jassem says good-bye and stands proudly smiling.

"Jassem, I am sorry I could not talk longer to your mother but I barely understood her. I am sure she felt the same way speaking to Pam and me."

We all begin laughing.

"Mrs. Williams, she is happy to hear your voices. It did not matter if no one understood. I have told her so much about Pam and your family."

"Pam tells me you are going home for a couple of weeks."

"Yes, Mrs. Williams."

"Well. Take care of yourself. I wish you a safe trip there and back. Please send my regards to your family."

"I will and thank you, Mrs. Williams."

When Momma leaves the room Jassem blows out a sigh of relief and hugs me.

"Oh I love you so much. Put on your shoes and let's go."

"Go where?"

"I don't know, anywhere."

We drive around and end up at McKellar Lake. I hadn't visited this lake for many years and initially doubted if I remembered the location. It is a huge lake with picnic tables, walking trails, and boat ramps. What a perfect day to stroll along the water. We find a nice spot and take off our shoes to feel the sand on our feet.

"So you are done packing for your trip."

"No. I will pack tonight. I don't plan to take much with me."

"Jassem, what are you going to tell your family and your fiancée, especially your fiancée? You knew sooner or later I was going to ask."

"I have an idea but honestly I don't know. Let's not talk about it now. Please! I only want us to have a pleasant day before I leave. No problems. Please!

"Jassem, you know we don't argue. But you are always the one insisting we communicate and talk everything out. Now is not the time to pick and choose because it is uncomfortable to discuss. We are at a fork in the road. Don't you think we had better talk about this some more?"

"Pam, you are correct but I don't have all the answers. I don't know what to say. I only know I need to return home so we will have a future together. If you were born in Kuwait this would be so much simpler. Wishful thinking I guess?"

"You are one of the most intelligent men I have ever met and you think matters out. Discussing us with your family, your superiors and who knows who else is an awful burden for one person. Not knowing exactly what's ahead is scaring me to death."

"Pam, this is why I love you so much. Why weren't you born in Kuwait?"

"Jassem, if God wanted me to be born in Kuwait, I would have. Our meeting that cold January night was no accident. God has a purpose for everything. He does."

"This is true. But Pam, again, I don't have all the answers and I don't wish to talk about her."

"Her. Hmmmm. Fine, Jassem we will not talk about it!"

"Pam, you know I will tell you everything when I come back. I will get permission for us to marry and we can begin planning our future. That will be only a formality. My parents know how we feel about each other and once I talk to them face to face, they too will understand."

If she loves Jassem as I do, losing him to another woman not to mention a non-Kuwaiti is going to be devastating and an embarrassment. I sympathize for this mysterious female but not having Jassem in my life is unimaginable.

We leave McKellar Lake and eat at a nearby seafood restaurant. Jassem wants me to return with him to the BOQ and offers to bring me back later in the evening. I decide to go home. Saying good-bye to him even for a week-or-so-long trip home is too much a test of the wills.

As evening descends, Jassem's demeanor changes to worry. I am on the verge of crying my heart out because something is not right. It's impossible to be specific but it's there. The eeriness is more like the quiet before a storm.

"Are you sure you don't want to go back with me? I will bring you back tonight."

"Jassem, that's too much. I would only be a distraction and besides you need to get up extra early tomorrow."

"If you say so. Two weeks will come and go before you know it and then I'll be back."

Jassem walks me to the back porch. We hug, which feels like an eternity, kiss, and he leaves. I decide not to go in but sit on the porch instead for a while. I wait all night and no call from Jassem. He is in deep thought as well.

Sunday, the next day

It is seven-fifteen and Daddy is in the bathroom shaving. Nuri and Jassem should be well on their way to the airport by now. Still no call.

"Hey there!"

Aunt Bell is leaning over the fence yelling through the boys' bedroom open window for someone to come and get two skillets of yeast biscuits. Felton, my youngest brother, hurries out the back door. She hands him our breakfast biscuits. I hold the door open as he walks up the steps. The aroma from the biscuits is delectable enough to eat uncooked. The phone rings. It must be Jassem.

"I got it! Hey Jassem! Good morning to you too! I love you more."

Jassem is calling from the airport and is about to board the plane. He was up most of the night and could not sleep.

"Please take care and I will see you when you get back. Good-bye."

What advice will his parents offer? Whoever this woman is, if she truly loves him, she'll not give him up without a fight. Why did he wait so long to tell me about her? Suppose he sees her and decides to say nothing? Or even worse, sees her and determines she should be his wife. After all, I am here and she is there.

Jassem's Return

What's going on with Jassem? Two long arduous weeks and still no word. I am positive everything is going the way we wish. On the other hand, I envision him and this woman sitting together privately, sharing her love for him and the future she dreams of.

The few words of Arabic I speak certainly would not help me if I called Kuwait. Does it matter? As soon as they hear my American voice they will assume it's me. Besides, I don't have a number. Why didn't I ask for a number to his parent's home? Or, why didn't he offer a number? I need to relax and wait. Aunt Bell always says, if you think long, you think wrong.

Vanessa and her friend Michelle are coming by shortly to pick me up so we can go to the International House of Pancakes at Union and Bellevue. Some Saturdays we end up there when we want to get out and not necessarily anywhere special.

Anyways, I am tired of thinking. I freshen up and wait for Vanessa on the back porch steps. Something is wrong with Aunt Bell's toilet and Daddy is under the house getting some tools. Our home was built with a storage space under the house. The only access is a small door near the back porch.

"Hey Daddy, it's me. I am waiting for Vanessa. We are going to the pancake house."

"Something's wrong with your grandmother's plumbing. She is just too hard on stuff. Every time I look around something is breaking."

"Oh well. I'm sorry," I say laughing.

"I wish she would listen. Can't tell her nothing."

"Daddy, gotta go! Vanessa is here. See you later."

Vanessa borrowed her father's car. He always checks for dings and scratches whenever she returns with it.

"Hey Vanessa. Hey Michelle."

"Hey Pam."

"Hello."

"What have you been up to Michelle?"

"Same ole, same ole."

Michelle is an attractive brown-skinned six-feet-tall young lady who changes wigs daily – with her favorite being an afro. She speaks 100 miles per minute and if you do not listen carefully, you literally will miss the conversation. She lives up the street from Vanessa and they've known each other since elementary school. Michelle and I have a less than tolerable relationship. Vanessa says she has been somewhat bitter, if not jealous, from the time Vanessa and I became close buddies.

The parking lot at IHOP is sparsely populated, which means faster service. The waitress greets us and says we can sit anywhere we want. She follows us with menus to a booth next to the parking lot. We tell her no need for menus because we know what we want to order.

"What can I get you girls?"

Michelle orders a Coke and apple pie, Vanessa hot tea and lemon pie, and I order hot tea and coconut cream pie – my absolute favorite. Small talk ensues and Michelle kept us drawn in with gossip about her latest boyfriend.

"Yeah, Pam. Vanessa tells me you are now messing around with an A-rab."

I look at Vanessa and smile.

"What is it with you? You hung out with that one white boy in high school and then there were those Nigerians a couple of years ago. You got problems with brothers?"

I take a deep sigh, "I declare. Drop it, Michelle."

"Hey, I am trying to keep it real. You know my sis-tah."

"Keep it real? I have no problem whatsoever with brothers. I am sought out. Okay."

"Yeah right!"

"Michelle. What do you know about A-rabs?"

"What do you mean? What do I know? I don't know nothing about those folk. And further more honey child, I really don't care to know."

"Exactly! You don't know nothing about Arabs so how can you even speak on it?"

"Like I said, I call them like I see them, and you act like you got problems with brothers. Or better still, you think you too good?"

That last comment infuriates me. "You know, Michelle, each and every time we have gotten together, which is very few, you either talk about my clothes, my hair, or my skin complexion. Now it's the men in my life. Look at yourself."

"Honey child that's right, look at me. I am fine. Ain't nothing wrong with me. You need to check yourself."

"Michelle, if you say anything else to me I am going to reach over this table and knock your nothing-wrong-with-me behind back to yesterday. I am sick of you talking about me all the time. One more word, Michelle!"

Michelle throws her fork down on the table, rolls her eyes at Vanessa and me, snatches up her purse, and leaves the table.

"I am leaving, Vanessa; I don't have to deal with your so-called friend."

"Michelle and Pam, please."

She walks to the public phone in the rear and takes out her coin purse to make a call.

"Pam, I declare!"

"Vanessa, I guess it's time to go! You know Michelle never cared for me and why do we have to pretend? I am not in the mood for this kind of crap."

Vanessa goes to console Michelle and to determine who she called. She is talking to her boyfriend to come and get her. Just in case she had a change of mind to hit me from behind or do something stupid, I get up and sit on the opposite side of the booth. She has a reputation of behaving nutty at times. Vanessa offers to take her home but she adamantly insists we leave her alone.

"Pam, let's go. Michelle is ticked off and is cussing like a sailor."

As soon as Vanessa and I got in the car we begin laughing hysterically and Vanessa can barely start the car.

"Pam, you know Michelle is a big crybaby and always

out there running her mouth. Would you have hit her with your coconut cream pie?"

"Girl, don't be crazy. I wouldn't waste my coconut cream pie on her. I would have used your lemon pie! I guess I will not be seeing Michelle anytime too soon!"

"Pam, she's mad at me too!"

In hindsight, I am glad Michelle was with us. I would have told Vanessa about Jassem's fiancée. Vanessa turned the volume up on her Johnny "Guitar" Watson eight-track and we bopped and sang all the way to Eloise Street.

Both of my parents' cars are in the drive so she parks on the street. We stretch out on the hood of the car and continue to listen to music. Marcus drives up. He has a little infatuation with Vanessa and never misses a moment to flirt.

The sun has gone down and a car pulls up in front of us and puts on the high beams. Who could be that rude? Someone steps out of the driver's side and turns the headlights off. It is Jassem. I dash off the car and run into his arms.

"When did you get back?"

"Early afternoon!"

"Why didn't you call me when you made it in?"

"Pam, I went straight to bed when I arrived at the BOQ I did call and spoke with your mother. She said you were not at home."

"Oh. I have been gone with Vanessa."

"Hello, Marcus and Vanessa."

"Hey, Jassem. How was Kuwait?" asks Marcus.

"Wonderful. Thank you."

"Glad you made it back, Jassem. I am sure you and

Pam have to catch up on things. I'll talk to you later, buddy."

"Thanks again, Vanessa," I say. "You know we need to find out what's up with Michelle."

"I plan to stop by her place and see how she's doing and tell her you apologized. All of this before Daddy's car inspection."

We all laugh. Marcus goes into the house and Vanessa drives away. Jassem turns the car around and parks in front of the house.

"Pam, I missed you so much."

"Jassem, I was going crazy?"

"I wanted to call but I decided it would be best to wait."

Jassem speaks of his mother and how she cried profusely when he walked in the house. She and family members had prepared all his favorite dishes. His father, siblings and relatives filled their home for days to hear him tell about his travels and especially America. He jokingly commented they treated him as though he is important.

All the while Jassem is sharing the highlights of home, the most critical appointment is not mentioned. This blatant evasiveness is the answer to the unasked question. He continues to talk and my worst fears are staring me in the face. I interrupt him.

"Stop, Jassem! If we were granted permission to marry it would have been the first thing out of your mouth when you saw me. But instead you talk around it. They said no. Didn't they?"

He holds me and whispers in my ear, "I tried. I am so sorry."

I begin to cry. "This is terrible. We don't have a chance or a future together. How can we?"

"Pam. Pam. Listen. It's not over. I can go to them again and ask. They will probably grant us the second time."

"Probably! Hmmm. Probably!"

With a deep sigh I hold his face in my hands and take a slow deep breath. "I know your touch. I know your smell."

"Pam, please don't do this. Please! Sometimes things in life come easy when others take time. Pam, you must be patient with our relationship. It's in Allah's hands."

Jassem takes a tissue and wipes my tears. He reaches for a towel in the back seat. Wrapped inside are two beautiful silver miniature bowls he brought me from home. They are used for burning incense. Sometimes Jassem burns frankincense in a similar bowl in his room.

He has a couple of Arabic eight-tracks from home and wants me to hear them. He is tired from his long journey and my eventful day has worn on me. We listen to the music until I notice Jassem's physical fatigue. I do not want him to fall asleep at the wheel, so I urge him to leave and call me when he makes it back to the base.

Not one mention of the mysterious fiancée. Jassem does not seem to understand this dismissive approach doesn't solve anything. It creates underlying suspicion. I've decided for the time being not to mention her again unless he raises the subject – probably never. Perhaps she did share her dreams with him.

The Departure

We have purposefully spent every day together since his trip home. We did not agree or disagree to see one another on such intense terms, it just happened. The uncertainty of our future compelled us to value time differently. He began seriously teaching me basic Arabic and I am now a stellar student. If our plans move forward and we are granted permission to marry, I will be permitted to practice my Christianity in private. This choice is better than not being able to worship at all.

These last couple of weeks have been magical with a slight eeriness. Jassem is insisting I remain positive with this process of permission. My gut feeling is telling me otherwise and still no mention of his fiancée. I am resolved to the reality of Jassem's overt idiosyncrasy of evasiveness. Going through the motions with no short-term plans is like a novice gambling it all away without a backup plan. We have none.

Oh how distressing to think that Jassem asked to marry me and my parents are ignorant of one of the most significant events in my life. Initially, upon my suggestion we agreed to the discretion due to complications of our circumstances. But now time has passed and our circumstances are the same. It hurts deeply to believe Jassem is unsure, if not doubtful of our future. Is he afraid of the possibility of embarrassing or failing me? God I pray I am so wrong in thinking he's riding the fence with two relationships – if so, chances are I am the loser. Simply, he's returning to Kuwait.

Unequivocally, I believe him when he says he could never love anyone after loving me. Lately, he often holds me as if it is for dear life.

Daddy's Aunt Othella in Jackson, Tennessee, has taken ill. He and Aunt Bell are planning to leave mid-morning and spend the day there. They probably will not return until late tonight. Jackson is 45 minutes east of Memphis.

Ironically, this is the day Jassem leaves Memphis. He has been transferred for a short duty of a couple of weeks in San Diego, then he will be leaving the States. The plan is for him to be here at one and for us to spend time together before he leaves on a red-eye flight. Daddy is in the carport under the hood of his car making a last-minute inspection. I walk to the back door.

"Daddy, what time are you leaving for Jackson?"

"Here shortly at eleven o'clock sharp. Why?"

"Can I go?"

"Sure you can. They will be glad to see you. Don't forget to grab a sweater. We may be back here late. Go tell your grandmother we will pick her up in front of the gate promptly at eleven."

After telling Aunt Bell, I rush back in order to put a new plan in place. This last day for Jassem in Memphis has played in my mind scenario after scenario. I will do what I believe he hasn't been able to do – let go. Leaving with Daddy is perfect.

I take a notepad and pen from the shelf in the dining room to write Jassem a farewell note.

> Jassem, love of my life,
>
> Please forgive me for not having the courage to see you. Your love for me is beyond anything I could ever imagine.
>
> Jassem, you took a turn which placed you on my path and I truly THANK God for that. Now it is time for you to return to your own intended journey.
>
> Remember, I know your touch and I know your smell.
>
> Thank you for loving me.
>
> Love,
> Pam

I rub the note on my chest then place it in an envelope. I wanted to write his name in Arabic but I didn't have time to do it correctly so I write it in English. Everyone in the house is gone but Melinda. I ask her to please make certain Jassem receives the envelope in his hand and to only tell him I went out of town with Daddy and Aunt Bell.

"Pamela Jean. Let's go!"

"I'm coming, Daddy."

I grab my sweater and leave out the front door. Daddy opens the back door for me and Aunt Bell yells from her drive for me to sit in the front. I put shades on and look ahead. This lump in my throat will soon leave.

I now begin a life without Jassem. As long as I live I will be thankful to him. I know a little more about the world, the people in it, and a foreign religion. In a few years we will be pleasant memories to each other. Oh God, how I want to scream and cry! Oh Jassem, how I love you so!

"Pam, why are you so quiet?" asks Daddy.

"Hmmm, nothing. Just enjoying the scenery on this pretty day."

"It is at that."

We arrive in Jackson and drive on a frontage road. This city is somewhat rural and much smaller than Memphis. Daddy makes a U-turn then a right into a dead-end street. I know little about these relatives. Daddy usually visits here alone. They live in a housing project that is really nice compared to others I've seen. We walk carefully down four concrete steps. There is a small vegetable garden with tomatoes and cabbage on the side of the porch. Roses line the short walkway to the door. Daddy softly knocks and an elderly woman walks up to the door and smiles. He holds the door open and we walk in. A flight of stairs to the left, and on the right is a small living room. It is filled with about six or so people, mostly elderly. Everyone exchanges greetings. Surely they all don't live here. Aunt Othella must be gravely ill. Two men get up and offer their seats to Aunt Bell and me.

"You must be Pam."

"Yes, ma'am."

"You don't know who I am. Do you?" she chuckles. "I am Tommie Lee's cousin Brenda. I've known him since he was knee high."

"Nice to meet you."

A young lady probably my age comes down the stairs. Cousin Brenda says it is her baby girl, Tasha. She is tiny, about my height, with a long ponytail down her back. An elderly gentleman peers from the stairs.

"Hey Bell and Tommie Lee. I saw you all drive up from the window. Come on up. Othella's going down and she ain't gonna recognize you. Tommie Lee, she your daughter?"

"Yes, that's my oldest girl Pam."

"Hello. She look just like Marjorie."

Daddy and Aunt Bell speak to this man known as Cousin Eugene. Daddy says I do not have to come upstairs, so I don't.

One of the ladies says there is plenty to eat and for me to wash my hands and make myself at home. Tasha and I go into the kitchen. She points to the baker's rack and asks me to turn the radio on low. A small table with three chairs is in front of a window next to the back door. The stove is covered with food. I wash my hands in the sink and walk over to the stove.

Tasha insists she prepare our plates. She places a modest portion of greens, potato salad, chow-chow, and smothered chicken with rice on my plate. She cuts a slice of caramel cake along with some smothered chicken on her plate. We both laugh because I tell her I also like to eat dessert with the main dish.

After eating, Tasha and I leave out the back to a really

nice community park across the street. Two young men and a young lady with a boom box are sitting on the park table near a huge magnolia tree. Tasha says she's known all of them her entire life and they are good friends.

It is ten after one. Jassem should have read the note by now. What have I done? This may not be a perfect plan but I am glad to be around strange people and not at home. They don't know my situation and can't judge or comment on it either way. Oh Jassem! It may take some time but we will both move on.

The young lady, Veronica, invites Tasha and me to her home. We read magazines, laugh about everything imaginable and listen to lots of music. Around six o'clock we leave Veronica's and head back. Tasha is finishing college in a couple of months and then she plans to go to law school. Her father died in Vietnam and her mom and Aunt Othella are sisters.

More relatives had come to the house and the men seem to be standing out front talking, including Daddy. Everyone else is in the living room engaged in soft conversations while listening to a Mahalia Jackson album. Tasha and I end up at the kitchen table again. I invite her to come to Memphis.

We leave Jackson for Memphis at seven-fifteen. Daddy takes his time driving back. I enjoyed meeting these relatives even under the distressing conditions.

It is mentally exhausting forcing back thoughts of Jassem and me all day. I cannot wait to talk to Melinda then go to bed. My heart is shattered.

Jassem arrived on time and Melinda handed him the envelope. He took the note, waited in the driveway a while, then left. Melinda said Jassem phoned at least a half a dozen times last night. Vanessa came by as well and seemed surprised to learn I left for Jackson. After church service tomorrow I'll go over and tell her Jassem's fiancée secret and why the change in plans today. She'll understand.

Incidents of Life

Someone is knocking at the door. Who is knocking on our door this early on a Sunday morning? Oh my goodness. It might be Jassem? Felton answers the door.

"Hey. What's going on?"

I could not make out who it is or what they are saying.

"Oh come on in."

I stand in the hall frozen as Felton opens the door. It is our neighbor, Eddie Lee. He wants to borrow Daddy's hair clippers for a couple of minutes. I sit on the edge of the bed and become ill. You fool, he's gone. At that point, I decide not to go to worship. I go back to bed ill.

Everyone has left for service and the house is empty. I prepare a hot bubble bath, sit in it and cry, cry, cry. In my lifetime I will never meet anyone like Jassem. Never! Where are you and is your mind kind to you?

I robe up and nervously clean sporadically, setting the table and prepping dinner. Out of respect for the Lord's Day we only listen to gospel but today, I am breaking the rules while no one is here. I locate the Temptations album and repeatedly play "Memories." The lyrics say it all.

I think I hear a car in the driveway and hasten to the front door. It is only someone turning around. What is wrong with me? He's gone. Sitting on the sofa I stare out, thinking this type of behavior will lead surely to some sort of mental illness if I don't get a handle on it.

It's time to call Vanessa. I will leave a message for her to call me when she returns from church. To my surprise Vanessa answers. She stayed out late and overslept. A cousin from Atlanta was in town and she came over yesterday to see me before they went out. Vanessa insists I explain why I went to Jackson and I reiterate it's best to tell her in person. She offers to come and pick me up right away. I tell her to have the tissue ready.

I cover the fresh cornbread I baked and write a note for Momma. Looking in the mirror I am pale with swollen eyes. I accidentally left the only pair of shades I own in Daddy's car. I do not want to look completely wretched so I apply a little eye shadow and foundation. As soon as I button my skirt Vanessa is in the drive blowing the horn. I slip on my sandals and lock the front door.

"Hey Vanessa, you know you my girl."

"No problem. What is going on with you? Didn't Jassem leave yesterday? Melinda told me you went to Jackson."

I start from the beginning with Jassem asking me to marry him and then the news about his fiancée. How his evasiveness wore on my faith, which prompted me to do something as drastic as going to Jackson. She conscientiously listens with bouts of sighs indicating incredulity.

Vanessa parks the car and takes her keys and wallet inside. We begin one of our long walks in the neighborhood and end up at the park. She makes no serious comment but reminds me how blessed I am to have met someone so special. She encourages me not to write him off in my future, despite his planned marriage. Also, avoid thinking negative.

"Pam you never know what God has planned for you and why out of all the people in the world you two met. I will not say anything to set you up for a letdown later but I don't think this is it. Maybe now you can concentrate on a singing career. You know I keep telling you, Pam, that's your ticket out of here."

"You are probably right about the singing but Vanessa honestly I don't know what to think anymore. I'm all thought out. "

"Girl I can't imagine. I'll leave you with this. My grandma Jenkins always says time takes care of it all."

It's warm, not too humid and I feel like walking back home. Vanessa walks with me to the overpass below the park and then we go our separate ways. It has been years since I last braved this three-mile walk.

When I make it home the Williams Sunday ritual is playing out – lounging after dinner. Momma and my sisters are in the bedroom talking and sharing the comic section of the newspaper. I tell them Jassem left yesterday and in a few weeks he will leave the States. They are all flabbergasted. Melinda did not realize it was her last time seeing him. Momma asks why I didn't let anyone know before now and if he would be coming back anytime soon. I merely reply, I really do not know. I hastily change the subject and ask Momma about leftovers from dinner. I eat and afterwards call Aunt Bell to ask if I can ride with her to evening service.

This is life without Jassem.

Three weeks later

No letter or phone call. It's the end of August and the heat coupled with humidity feels like an open oven. This prompts me to hose down the carport and it is now cool and refreshing. Earlier I grabbed a few blackberries and luscious peaches from the orchard and sliced them. Thalia is walking down the street probably from her mom's. I call her over.

"Hey Thalia!"

"Can you believe I had to go up to ma dear's in this hot butt sun to get a cup of flour? I'm frying some chicken for dinner."

"Thalia, sit down and cool off."

"I can't. I'm watching the boys and you know what that means."

"Okay!"

"Pam isn't that your cousin Rajean walking up the street in a hurry? Where is she going in this heat?"

"Rajean!" I yelled.

"Hey Pam. I've got a bus to catch."

"Where are you going?"

"To midtown."

"Come over and cool off. Catch the next one."

Rajean looks at her watch, stops and takes up the offer. She is wearing a matching black and lavender African head wrap and dress.

"Rajean, how do you keep those clothes on in this heat?" laughs Thalia.

"Honey child don't you know? I am cooler than the both of you. This is cotton and it repels heat."

"Okay! Whatever!" says Thalia.

As usual Rajean invites me to go to the health food store. I complain the heat is draining all my energy and I am not up to riding a bus to mid-town. As she hoses off her feet I go inside to get her a cold glass of water. Momma overhears our conversation and offers me the car to take Rajean to midtown. I need to be back at least by three o'clock. She has somewhere to go. I jokingly ask Thalia to join us. This is the middle of a hot day and she unwaveringly prefers activities after sunset. Rajean and I deal with the heat favorably. Finally, I will see the place that Rajean deems a lifeline to perfect health.

She knows more about midtown than south Memphis. I always considered it to be a marijuana-smoking "hippie" hot spot. Quaint mom-and-pop shops are everywhere. I park down the street from an old Victorian home turned health store. There are lots of plants and wind chimes complementing this charming little structure. A natural drink bar and specialty foods are downstairs. The shop has a welcoming ambiance. Bamboo chairs and tables are located in the center with a ceiling fan overhead.

A young lady behind the counter preparing the drinks immediately recognizes Rajean. She is a tall young lady with long brown wavy hair past her hips and a white bandana tied around her head. She has on jeans and a long baby pink wrap-around blouse. It is difficult to determine her ethnicity.

The heat is taking a toll on me. I need a cool drink and somewhere to sit for a moment.

"Hey Tina." says Rajean happily.

"Nice to see you ladies. I will be with you in a moment."

"Oh honey child take your time. I am here with my cousin Pam."

"Hello Pam."

"Hi Tina."

Rajean picks up a small shopping basket and starts filling it with natural fig energy bars and banana nut bread. She walks to the counter and orders drinks for us.

"Pam, I told her to put some bee pollen in yours for energy. Don't worry. It's all natural and it will give you an energy boost."

"Oh I know, all healthy."

"Girl you just got a love hangover. Don't be shame. It's only natural."

I smile and sit back in the comfortable chair. Tina walks over with our drinks.

"Yes, Rajean and I go way back. She is a good friend and such a faithful customer. Pam, I put a double shot of bee pollen in it for you. No charge. Relax, take your time, and enjoy the shop. When is your baby due?"

"What did you say?" I said.

"A baby! That's what's wrong with you. Tina not only specializes in herbs but she is also a bona-fide psychic. And she gets paid for it. Trust me. Just think. You got this one for free," laughs Rajean.

I am in complete disbelief.

"Oh Pam. You didn't know?"

Tina sits down and takes my hands. "Pam, you have so many good spirits around to guide and protect you. Many! You are going to have a beautiful baby girl. Ah! Don't worry. Her father's love for you will never cease. Never! Congratulations."

Am I pregnant? How did she know anything about Jassem? Can this get any worse? Rajean gets up and rubs my back.

"Thank you, Tina. My cousin will be fine. See about your customers. Take a deep breath, Pam, and drink your juice. I know you are in shock. Your baby is a blessing."

"Rajean, Jassem is gone and now I am pregnant. My parents are going to flip completely out, especially Daddy."

"Pam, stop worrying so much. This will be a shock to everyone but they will get over it. Trust me."

"I need to take a pregnancy test. When we leave here I am going by the drug store."

"Why are you wasting your money? Tina told you what's going on."

"Rajean, I am going by the drug store."

She leaves me downstairs and continues shopping throughout the entire shop. My mind keeps drawing a blank. No wonder I am fatigued. I have been so consumed with him being gone I neglected to listen to my body.

Tina returns to check on me and apologizes again. I reassure Tina the news was better received here with my cousin, in this environment and sitting in a comfortable chair, than in a doctor's office alone. I decide to purchase some bee pollen and tell her I plan to return in the future with Rajean.

As planned I stop by the Rexall drugstore and buy a pregnancy kit. Next door to the drugstore is a Mobil gas station where I replace the gas we used for midtown.

When we arrive home, Rajean stays to see if Tina was on point. After Momma leaves, I hurry into the bathroom and take the test. I sit on the edge of the tub and place the kit on top of the toilet seat. The applicator turns bright pink with a plus sign. Suddenly, I feel calm, surreal and almost euphoric. Jassem and I are having a baby. I open the door and whisper to Rajean, "Girl, I am pregnant for real!"

"I told you Tina knows her stuff. So you are going to have a little Kuwaiti. Remember she said a baby girl."

"What am I going to do? What do I do now, Rajean?"

"Give yourself a couple of days for this to sink in. Then, tell Aunt Marjorie. Oh before I forget. I bought you a little something from the store. It's cocoa butter oil for your breasts and stomach so you don't get stretch marks. Start using it now."

"Wait a minute. You bought this oil before you knew?"

"No. You got it wrong. I bought the oil when I knew. Girl, take this oil. I am going home now."

"Thanks, Rajean, for everything and I mean everything. By the way, Tina is good people."

With a handful of magazines I head back to the carport. Every thought imaginable as to what my future would be races in sections through my head. Jassem, I can't have this baby by myself.

Daddy drives up and a lump is in my throat. He is going to be completely disappointed. He warned me but I did not listen. He asks how am I doing and I tell him fine.

I head out the back yard through the orchard to go to Aunt Bell's. To be near my grandmother is comforting. I close the gate latch and a car drives up – it looks like

Vanessa's. I don't remember her telling me she was coming over.

"Vanessa. Vanessa. I'm back here. Where are you on your way?"

"I was going home but something told me to stop by here. I'm not kidding."

"This has been a weird day. Girl, I mean weird."

"What's up?" asks Vanessa.

"Vanessa, walk with me. Momma is making a peach pie tonight and I need to get some peaches. And, whatever you do don't get excited. Remember don't get excited. Vanessa, I am pregnant."

"What!"

"God bless America. Shhhhh."

"Pam, you are pregnant. Are you sure?"

"I took a pregnancy test a little while ago."

"Pam, you never told me you thought you could be pregnant."

"I took the test today after a psychic told me I was pregnant. She is a friend of my cousin Rajean."

"A psychic! Girl, you don't believe in those kind of folk. Oh my God."

"Oh Vanessa. It's a long story."

"Do you want to go somewhere and talk? Are you hungry? I am!"

"Okay. Let's go and get something to eat after I pick these peaches for Momma."

Vanessa helps me pick peaches and afterwards we dine at a Chinese restaurant on Elvis Presley Boulevard. She placidly listens as I methodically share the events of the day. Vanessa has an unfailing ability to speak caring words of wisdom and today her compassion calms my spirit and the looming fear vanishes. She agrees with Rajean to postpone telling my parents immediately or at least until I sort my troubling thoughts.

At The Graveside

Aunt Bell's youngest brother, Walter, died suddenly from a heart attack. He was the uncle who constantly smiled, married who knows how many times and never spoke an unkind word to anyone – even when wronged. He has sixteen children from his marriages and otherwise. Relatives from Detroit, Michigan, and as far as Buffalo, New York, arrive in town to pay their respects. Uncle Walter was never affiliated with any congregation and Aunt Josephine, his widow, will hold a graveside service.

Coincidentally, this is the week I decide to face my fears and tell Momma. I am becoming increasingly apprehensive and this secret is wearing me down. I need to be under a doctor's care and soon the pregnancy will become difficult to hide. Jassem, where are you? What could I have done differently to prevent where I am now? Going down to Jackson did not help matters at all. Goodness, another bout of foolish thinking. The result is still the same, pregnant.

With trepidation, I walk into the living room where Momma is in good spirits polishing the furniture.

"It's amazing how you can polish one day and the next day dust is right back." she says.

"Momma. I'm pregnant."

She keeps polishing without looking up.

"Pam, I've been knowing that. I was just waiting for you to tell me."

"You knew. How did you know?"

"I am your mother. Mothers know these things. It's a shame Jassem is not here. That young man should be with you now. And still no word from him, huh?"

"No."

"Does he know?"

"No, Momma."

"Lord help! I pray to God you hear from him. That child is going to need a daddy. We need to get you in to see Dr. Randolph soon. How are you feeling?"

"Fine."

"This is going to kill Tommie Lee."

Not saying another word, she continues moving articles from the table to polish. I go to the bedroom and stretch across the bed feeling partially relieved. Momma not becoming hysterical is a scenario I never imagined. Why is she so calm? I can only assume her disappointment occurred sometime ago when she earlier suspected my pregnancy and dealt with it then. Perhaps Momma's empathy lies with the grief of her eldest daughter's dishonorable and heart-wrenching circumstance of being pregnant and the father is gone.

"Pam, here is the number to Dr. Randolph's office. Call him and make an appointment for next week. No need for you to sit around and feel sorry for yourself. What's done is done. Think about the baby."

She hugs me. This is another example of why I love

our mother so dearly. She unconditionally loves us. Only a mother's wisdom can recognize when to push and when to pull away from a situation.

Aunt Bell calls later and asks if anyone is interested in riding with her to North Memphis to drop off food and sodas to Aunt Josephine. Felton and I decide to go. Aunt Bell hardly cared for any of Uncle Walter's wives after the first one. Felton asks, why are we going over to drop off food to Aunt Josephine's and you don't like the woman. Aunt Bell casually replies, in life you sometimes may not care to do things but you do them for peace sake. We literally walk in, drop off the food and leave. No socializing whatsoever.

Saturday morning

Today there is overcast. Daddy mowed the lawn at sunrise so that he can make it to Uncle Walter's 10:00 a.m. service on time. It's being held at a cemetery in Collierville, a small town east of Memphis. Daddy spent most of his youth there and attended a one-room schoolhouse.

We need to arrive at Aunt Josephine's around 9:30 a.m. to participate in the funeral procession. Marcus stops by momentarily and all of us are purposely riding with him, with the exception of our parents. He has a laid-back demeanor and drives as such. Daddy is quite the other extreme. On occasion when we were late for a function, Daddy had us almost in tears covering our eyes while he sped through the streets ducking and dodging as if he was on a speedway. Hopefully today a somewhat grieved frame of mind will sway his driving.

There are approximately 100 or so people here for the service. Throughout the cemetery are marble benches and a gazebo. Seating is limited to a few chairs and those standing are scattered about. Marcus and I are standing two rows behind our parents. Daddy's only sister, Aunt Laura Lee, flew in from San Francisco and she is standing next to him. During the prayer Momma turns around and looks at me, then whispers to Daddy. He discreetly turns and the appearance on his face speaks disbelief – she told him. Marcus nudges me and asks what is going on with our parents and why is Daddy constantly staring at me. I whisper to him Momma just told him I am pregnant. He nonchalantly shrugs his shoulders and says that shouldn't surprise anyone. You were with that brother 24/7. I shove him for that comment.

Moments later the service ends. To think we were only here for a short fifteen minutes, if that. Walking back to the car someone taps my left shoulder. It is Aunt Laura Lee. She embraces me.

"Hey, Pam."

"Hey, Aunt Laura Lee."

"So you are the one that pushed Uncle Walter out. Congratulations."

"I guess."

How do I respond to this remark? Is she being facetious or rudely sarcastic? It is another old cultural belief that in a family when someone is pregnant, it pushes another life out.

Everyone is heading to North Memphis to eat and do a little folk instigating. Uncle Walter's first wife, Aunt Edna Ruth, and his oldest stepdaughter live next door to

Aunt Josephine. This has always been cause for an uncomfortable situation.

Many years ago, the area was farmland and undeveloped. Uncle Walter and Aunt Edna Ruth married and built their gorgeous ranch-style home, complete with a couple of cows and chickens.

Aunt Edna Ruth had a daughter Connie Mae, prior to marrying Uncle Walter. Connie Mae married somewhat young and built a home next door. Her husband was killed in an automobile accident a few years after their marriage. When Aunt Edna Ruth and Uncle Walter divorced, she moved in next door with her daughter. Through the years fights and gun threats ensued – always about the children and new wives. But the feuding is about to take on a new twist. The deed for the house Aunt Josephine has lived in for over forty years as her home undeniably indicates the property owner to be Uncle Walter – also, Aunt Edna Ruth.

Gossip is looming that Aunt Edna Ruth wants her home back.

The Blessing

I'm a little over eight months pregnant and my baby girl is due March 31. I have named her Jannah and Momma is figuring out a middle name.

Every day I have looked in the mailbox for a letter from Jassem hoping he would at least tell me how he is living his life – and still nothing. And after all this time, knocking on the door still causes my heart to flutter with blind anticipation.

Daddy has not held a conversation with me since Uncle Walter's service. He speaks but makes it well known he does not have words for me. It is complicated living in my father's home with so much enmity.

Walking around this one-mile track every week at the junior high school I attended as a teenager is exercise and solace. Planning a new life for Jannah and me is the objective. I don't wish to remain in Memphis and I yearn for a new start somewhere, anywhere. However, options are limited with little money and no close relatives to jumpstart this inspiration. For whatever reason,

Jassem has decided to not communicate with me. I know he is praying or has prayed on my behalf. God hears my prayers and something better is being prepared for us. I feel it.

In the distance walking through the fence is Rajean.

"Hey Rajean. Stop rushing. Where am I going to run off to with this load?" I shout.

As she walks across the field I continue towards the play area and sit in a swing.

"Hey Pam. Aunt Marjorie told me you were probably here."

"Trying to get some exercise in for a healthy baby girl and stretched-out body. I haven't seen you in a while. What's going on with you?"

"Staying busy, that's all. Pam, you have been on my mind lately. After the baby is born, why don't you send Jassem some pictures? Didn't you say he gave you his father's address?"

"He sure did. His father works at the Kuwait Ministry Broadcast. I am glad I memorized the address. Rajean, that's an excellent idea."

"I want to make certain you are covering all bases. After your baby is born, I will assist you in communicating with the Kuwait Embassy and the State Department in D.C."

"Why those two places? And, why would they help me? Remember we were not married and that makes a big difference. Don't you think?"

"Your reason will be here in a couple of weeks, that's why. The State Department is there to assist Americans and the Embassy will assist you with him. Trust me that

Embassy has information on every Kuwaiti who sets foot on American soil. They may even know about you."

"Right, Rajean. A poor little black girl like me?"

"My people will never understand what this government and others mind you are capable of doing."

Rajean's vast knowledge and opinion about various subjects often leaves me paranoid or filled with misplaced thoughts. Somewhere in the bible it does state wisdom brings with it sorrow.

Her father, Uncle Sylvester, is barbecuing chitterlings for dinner. I am not a big fan of this pork delicacy, however, the cravings lately are erratic. We stop by the house to tell Momma I will be over there for a while to eat.

It is the morning of March 31 and not one contraction. Sleeping is no longer a possibility so I stare at the ceiling most nights. Vanessa and my friends gave me a baby shower with a bassinette full of newborn toiletries and toys for Jannah. I don't walk the track anymore in fear of labor beginning away from home. I spend a considerable amount of time reading on the back porch.

Vanessa, Rajean, and I are all sitting in the living room for the magic moment. Jannah seems quite content and relaxed, kicking my ribs. At 10:00 p.m. I send them home.

Friday, April 6, before morning I walk to the kitchen for a glass of apple juice and my water breaks. I begin to feel serious discomfort afterwards. I tell Momma and we prepare for the hospital. My sister Carolyn looks at me and begins to cry.

"Carolyn! What in the world is wrong with you? Why are you crying?"

"I am going to miss you and I will stick by you forever in my life."

"Oh! Carolyn, it's okay. Do me a favor and make sure the room is ready when I get back with your new little niece. And, don't forget to say a prayer."

"Pam. I will stick with you forever."

Evidently, she doesn't have a favorable view of a hospital or it is the expression on my face when the contraction hits. Before Momma and I get in the car, I ask Carolyn to call Vanessa and Rajean. Dear God, Daddy is in his bedroom and doesn't come out during all the commotion of me leaving. Oh Daddy!

The check-in process goes smoothly and I have a private room at St. Joseph Hospital. The nurse attaches a belt with a device around my stomach to monitor the baby's activities. It's nine o'clock and Dr. Townsend, my obstetrician, arrives. He examines me and I am barely dilated. Momma is nervously popping gum and leaves the room to smoke. The contractions are unbearable and Dr. Townsend will not give me anything for the pain.

Seven hours later and after another exam by Dr. Townsend, I am only dilated one half centimeter. This continues throughout the night and it is Saturday, two o'clock in the morning. I can no longer take the pain. I snatch the belt off my stomach, sit up and begin to moan loudly. Someone down the hall is wailing and I can't tolerate it. A nurse rushes in the room and is livid with me.

"Ms. Williams, you can't take this monitor off."

"This is pressing against my navel and it hurts. I am tired. I have been in pain for almost a day. I want my Momma."

"I am sorry but babies come when they want to and that's the way it is. Your Momma can not help you have this baby. Please do not take this off again. I will bring you some ice water. Dr. Townsend is here delivering a baby and when he is done, he will be here to see you."

She refastens the belt, rubs my forehead with a damp towel, and goes to get Momma from the waiting room. Momma walks in and looks exhausted.

"Pam. Why did you take the monitor off? You can't be doing things like that. Your doctor will be in shortly to see you. This is a shame they allow you to be in labor almost a day. He needs to do something."

"I can't take this pain. Did you hear that girl screaming?"

"Are you kidding? The entire hospital can hear her. She is a fourteen-year-old from Mississippi with a waiting room full of relatives."

Momma readjusts the bed and sits in the room with me. Dr. Townsend arrives and read the print-out on the machine. After another exam, I am dilated two and a half centimeters.

"Ms. Williams hang in there. The baby is in position but you need to dilate several more centimeters. She'll be here soon."

"I am tired, Dr. Townsend."

"I know but hang in there, young lady, you will be fine."

Thirty-two hours later and I am wiped out. Dr. Townsend returns for a third time and after this exam he has a worried look on his face. He tells me I need an emergency caesarean and I am rushed to the operating room. Jannah has turned around and is entangled in the umbilical cord. During the surgery, Dr. Townsend slightly cuts her face below the left eye with an instrument, possibly because the cord is around her neck. At 3:35 p.m. Jannah is born, 6 pounds and 7 ounces.

It seems he had to perform two emergency caesareans at nearly the same time. He cut another infant on the top of her head. Momma and the grandmother of the other nicked baby girl were looking through the window at the newborns. And determined the two newborn girls with adhesive bandages on the injured areas are the ones that were under the mercy of the doctor. The other grandmother cursed profusely about the incident but is thankful Dr. Townsend delivered two healthy baby girls.

After a few hours in recovery I am returned to my room filled with flowers and balloons. The nurse takes my temperature and it is above normal. I ask her to bring my baby to me and she declines because of the fever.

Day three and I have yet to see Jannah because of my fever. This catheter is irritating and tomorrow the nurses plan to get me out of bed and move about. Momma, a couple of her friends, and Vanessa are describing Jannah and that doesn't settle well with me – it isn't natural. All describe her as a little doll, extremely fair skin with long straight black hair.

Today I have a plan to see Jannah. The nurse typically comes in around seven in the morning to check vitals. I plan to chew as much ice as I can before she arrives.

"Good morning, Ms. Williams. How are you feeling? I am Mrs. Stevenson and I will be your nurse for today. Is there anything I can get for you?"

"Yes. My baby."

"Your chart indicates you have had a fever and for medical

reasons we can't allow you in contact with your baby until it is normal. I will check it and see where we are."

I have ice barely melted in my mouth and I take a silent gulp. She places the thermometer in my mouth. I will roll out of this bed if she asks if I'd eaten ice.

"Oh Ms. Williams, do you want to see your baby?"

"Yes!"

"Not a problem. Your temperature is normal. After I empty this catheter and get you cleaned up, I will get your baby."

A knock on the door and it is housekeeping to clean.

The room is now quiet again and I sit patiently in silence. The door gradually opens and Nurse Stevenson has Jannah. The caesarean has temporarily caused me to lose strength in my arms and Nurse Stevenson asks which side would I prefer to hold her on? I respond, the right please. She gently places her in my arms, lays the call buzzer on my shoulder, and leaves.

She is amazingly beautiful, healthy, and looks like a toy doll. I kiss her and cry. I begin to talk to her and she responds to my voice by squirming. Jassem, look what you've missed. I wish you were here. Thank you, Lord, for this blessing.

Saturday, April 14, at 9:15 a.m.

I leave St. Joseph Hospital with my new baby and a renewed sense of being. From this day forward I will do all in my power with God's help to ensure she has a quality life. Amen.

As Momma drives into the carport, all my sisters

eagerly come out to greet us. Jannah is snugly wrapped in a pink blanket Aunt Laura Lee sent from San Francisco. They all crouch at the car door taking my small suitcase, newborn gift package from the hospital, and other items. The back steps will be difficult for me with the twenty-seven stitches in my stomach. Momma carries Jannah, and I walk up the front porch steps.

All of the family including Aunt Bell are sitting in the living room admiring Jannah and taking turns holding her. Aunt Bell advises me not to hold Jannah so much because it will spoil her. I literally ignore the remark. I plan to be a mother who holds and loves her baby at each and every opportunity.

While I am lying in bed before retiring for the night, Daddy quietly walks into the room. Jannah is sleeping in the bassinette. He removes her blanket, rubs her head, and kisses both hands.

"Pam. This is a fine little girl."

"Thank you, Daddy. I think so too!"

"How are you doing?"

"I'm okay, Daddy. Thanks for asking."

He smiles and leaves.

Months of hurtful antagonism end with a blessed reassurance of Daddy's love for me and now for his granddaughter, Jannah.

The State Department and the Kuwait Embassy

Saturday, Memorial weekend 1979, smoke-filled grills and fire pits with barbecue are saturating the air throughout the neighborhood. Aunt Bell is making home-made ice cream and Momma is preparing banana puddings. Outside music boxes outplay one another with the soulful sounds of Memphis.

Daddy washed the carport and now it is lined with lawn chairs. Neighbors next door and several houses down are all in view enjoying the day. Marcus and his wife, Anne, arrive with her famous deviled eggs. Today, I choose to embrace the present pleasantries and tomorrow will be here soon enough.

Rajean is rubbing Jannah over her shoulder. I attentively take notes as she talks. She kept her word to assist me with locating Jassem or at best, getting a message to him. I now have the addresses and phone numbers of the Kuwait Embassy and the State Department. Rajean insisted I be specific with the requests and exercise careful selection of tone and words in dealing with both organizations. I plan to begin communicating on Tuesday. I will call the State Department and write the Embassy once I establish a contact.

The weekend was perfect. Locating Jassem is a necessity for his daughter's sake. I call the State Department and, as Rajean advised, request to speak to someone regarding a personal/domestic issue. Three transfers later, I speak to a Mr. Joseph Horowitz. He explains the limits of the State Department for a couple of vital reasons. One, we were not married, and two, Jassem is a foreign national. The ten-minute communication ended with a statement that the United States has no jurisdiction over the matter. He is sending me a list of Kuwaiti lawyers who practice in Kuwait that the State Department has classified as legitimate representatives. This was educational but less than beneficial. The idea of me hiring a Kuwaiti attorney is impossible.

The following Friday I receive a postcard from the State Department with a list of six Kuwaiti attorneys typed on the back. Only two have phone numbers. How utterly impersonal? What or how was I expecting the information? Perhaps, I expected Mr. Horowitz to send a sealed envelope and not an information-revealing postcard. This list may prove valuable in the future, but presently, I will keep it in a safe place.

The only hope remaining is to convince the Kuwait Embassy I desperately require assistance. I call and am given the name Colonel Ali Al-Khader in the Kuwait Liaison Office. I will send a letter prior to speaking with Colonel Al-Khader. If Rajean is correct, which she is most of the time, giving him all pertinent information prior to speaking with him allows time for pre-discussion research.

THE DEPARTMENT OF STATE
WASHINGTON, D.C. 20520

Overseas Citizens Services

{OVER}

Dear Miss Williams:

As per our conversation this morning attached is

a "lost of attorneys" in Kuwait one of which may

be helpful to you. I am sorry we were not able to

be of more assistance.

Sincerely,

T.R.N.

The correspondence hopefully will legitimize our conversation. I spend two days writing and rewriting a three-page letter. The beginning of July I will follow-up.

Three weeks after sending Colonel Al-Khader a letter, I receive an official letter indicating he is in receipt of my correspondence and the Kuwait Embassy is currently investigating the matter. And, to please call in the interim if I so desired. My spirit is telling me to be still and follow-up later.

August 12, 1979, I call Colonel Al-Khader. He recognizes my name and the receptionist transfers the call. He is professional and cordial, like all the Kuwaitis I'd come across. He places me on hold and returns, speaking in an unofficial manner.

"Ms. Williams, we have a delicate situation here. I believe your story. However, Lieutenant Al-Hashash is currently married and for other reasons I am not at liberty to disclose, it is complicated. I have spoken with his superiors and again, I reiterate this is a sensitive matter. Please understand the Embassy's position and know we want to do what is best for both parties involved. Ms. Williams, are you there?"

"Yes."

The news of Jassem's marriage is not what I expected, though deep inside, I knew. Hearing it from someone as neutral as a Kuwaiti Liaison Officer is traumatizing. My cheerful voice dissipated to sighs and speechlessness.

"Ms. Williams, I apologize profusely for giving you this news but believe me, I will be diligent in my efforts to convey your concerns to Lieutenant Al-Hashash."

"Thank you, Colonel Al-Khader."

"Did you know of his marriage?"

"I knew of his engagement when he left Memphis but Colonel Al-Khader, he did not know I was pregnant with his daughter."

"I see."

"Again, Ms. Williams, you have my word. I will assist you as best as humanly possible. Have a good afternoon, Ms. Williams."

"Good-bye, Colonel Al-Khader."

He moved on with his life and I will do the same. I only desire for him to know and at least acknowledge her existence. That is the least Jassem can do. Jannah is his first born, not the child his wife will probably give him.

September's orange and red colorful leaves and windy days arrive. Jannah looks identical to Jassem's niece I saw in a photo. She only has my fair complexion. Her features are distinctively Arab. Oh how he would so adore her!

It is four o'clock eastern time. With no communication from Colonel Al-Khader, it's time for me to follow up with a call.

"Good afternoon, may I please speak to Colonel Al-Khader?"

"Good afternoon. Who's calling please?"

"Ms. Pamela Williams from Memphis, Tennessee."

"One moment ma'am."

I do hope at least Jassem knows he has a daughter now. What a relief that would be.

"Ms. Williams."

"Hello, Colonel Al-Khader."

"No. This is Colonel Al-Alhoum. Colonel Al-Khader no longer works here."

"When…"

Colonel Al-Alhoum interrupts me and with an authoritative voice he says, "Ms. Williams I am aware of your situation and unfortunately, the Kuwait Embassy can no longer assist you. I am sorry. I wish you success in your efforts."

"What about Mr. Al-Hashash's knowledge of his daughter?"

"Ms. Williams, the Kuwait Embassy is unable to assist you. Have a pleasant afternoon. Good-bye."

What happened to Colonel Al-Khader? Why was this other Colonel curt and blatantly rude? Who is Jassem? No, who am I?

Dear God how I wish I was wealthy. I would fly to Kuwait with Jannah and wait for him in his living room with his wife.

Thank you, the United States State Department and the Kuwait Embassy, for an overindulgence in reality. We are on our own.

EMBASSY OF THE STATE OF KUWAIT
KUWAIT LIAISON OFFICE

3500 INTERNATIONAL DRIVE, N.W., WASHINGTON, D.C. 20008 • TEL: (202) 364-2200, 364-2215/16 • FAX: (202) 363-5846, 364-2241

Ref. No. : KLO ▮▮▮▮▮▮

Ms. Pamela J. Williams
▮▮▮▮▮▮▮▮▮▮▮▮▮▮▮▮▮▮▮▮▮▮

Dear Ms. Williams:

This is in reference to your letter dated ▮▮▮▮▮▮▮▮▮▮▮

As we advised you, we have referred and sent all prior correspondence to the Ministry of Defense for investigation. ▮▮▮▮▮▮▮▮▮▮▮▮▮▮▮▮▮▮▮▮▮▮▮▮▮▮▮▮▮▮▮▮▮▮▮▮▮▮ relationship with you.

We regret that we could not be of further assistance due to above reason.

Sincerely yours,

Chief, Kuwait Liaison Office

Suspicion

October 1979. Momma and I are talking at the dinner table. She is marinating meat and peeling potatoes for Sunday dinner. Jannah is gnawing on a stuffed toy. She is a healthy, playful six-month-old.

Rajean knocks on the back door and joins us. She brings me a couple of sassafras sticks for tea. It is a favorite flavor of mine and I appreciate her sharing. Momma heats up the tea kettle and Rajean goes in the hall to use the telephone. Tina from the health food store is extremely ill and Rajean is calling a friend to pick her up from our home so they can visit her at the hospital tonight.

Rajean returns to the dining area with her hands resting on her hips. We stare in anticipation of news she received while talking.

"Son of a guns!"

"Rajean, what happened?" asks Momma.

"Aunt Marjorie and Pam, your phone is tapped."

I exhale a sigh of relief with this joke. Momma looks peevishly at Rajean and says, "Girl, stop carrying on like that. You hear me."

"I was talking to a friend, Lester, and loud clicking and echoing is on your line. That's how you can tell someone is listening in. Please tell me you have not heard it. I hung up and called Lester again and still that mess was on the line. You are not on a party line."

Momma and I look at each other despondently.

"Rajean, that clicking doesn't mean anything. It could very well be trouble with our line."

"Pam, I suspect when you contacted the State Department and the Kuwait Embassy, regardless of your innocence and intent, it probably alerted some folk. Don't trip! You did your due diligence. I am going to say it again. The phone is tapped. I bet my life on it!"

"Okay, Rajean, that's enough." replies Momma.

"This government does whatever it chooses to do. And, I would not worry too much. This church-going family doesn't have anything to hide. When you hear it, call them on it. Say something like, I know you are listening and get off our line. That is your right as an American citizen."

"Rajean, I said enough."

"Okay."

Momma is upset. I on the other hand don't know what to believe. We continue to play with Jannah as if the last couple of minutes never took place. The kettle is whistling and Rajean prepares us a cup of tea.

We love Rajean and over the years have listened to her advice and cautions on matters. However, this surpasses menacing. If our line is tapped there is nothing we can do. Why would anyone want to listen to us, to me?

Lester comes by and picks up Rajean. Momma avoids discussing our telephone. Daddy arrives later and Momma calls him in the room and closes the door. I listen carefully but only hear mumbles. She returns to the kitchen not saying a word.

Were Rajean's suspicions correct or has she stepped into a sphere of lunacy?

I no longer desire to live in Memphis and consistently have felt this way prior to the birth of Jannah. I don't wish to raise her here, especially on Eloise Street. What can I do?

Georgia, a family friend from church, babysat us as kids. Her husband was murdered and she moved to Phoenix, Arizona. She was here for Christmas and spoke of the opportunities available there. Georgia said I would have no problem finding a good job to support Jannah and me. I want a fresh start but Phoenix isn't next door. It is across the country and mostly desert. Taking her up on the offer of moving there means Jannah and I will be alone with no close relatives.

Our parents have trusted Georgia for years. She has a heart of gold and is a "sign carrying" activist supporting anything she believes to be unfairly treated. God, please let me know if I should make this move to Phoenix. Amen.

July 1981. Jannah and I spend time at Vanessa's this afternoon. When I arrive home, a large envelope from Georgia is on the bed. I open the package and a note is taped to what appears to be the Sunday classified section of an Arizona paper, The Phoenix Sun. The note reads…

Time to make a move! Now pick your job! Start a new life for you and Jannah! There is page after page of want ads. Waiting for a perfect scenario may never arrive. It is time for me to move. I need to set a date and leave with the money I saved from working my part-time jobs.

Momma looks to see what Georgia sent and I share the paper and note with her. She admits that thoughts of Jannah and me leaving are bittersweet. Reminding me that faith in God and gumption can carry me through anything. I am completely taken by surprise when she adamantly suggests leaving Jannah with the family until I find a job, then fly her out later. She says this is one less issue to concern myself with while getting established.

I write Georgia the next day to see if the end of the summer will work for her and tell her that I plan to be alone. I have never flown on a plane and I don't feel adventurous. I'd prefer to travel on the bus and see the countryside.

September 1981. I leave for Phoenix tomorrow after-noon at three-thirty. All the sad good-byes and well wishing are over. Jannah will not understand why I am leaving her behind but I am praying our separation is short. She is loved so much and Momma is correct to leave her until I secure a job. To imagine me being in this position is unfathomable. A single mother, struggling to find herself and oh how about a relationship ending this way. God, all I ever dreamt in life was to get an education, marry a God-fearing man, and take care of him and a house full of children. Well, maybe this dream will happen later.

Marcus is taking me to the bus station shortly. Daddy is not at home to see me leave. He talked to me last night about discerning people and not to trust as easily as I have in the past. I know the origin of those thoughts. Carolyn made me one of her infamous cards with her favorite saying, "I will stick by you forever." Jannah is sensing our separation. All day she has not let me out of her sight.

Marcus quietly takes the luggage out the back door to avoid Jannah seeing it. I discreetly kiss everyone and all of a sudden Jannah begins to scream and cry. I can't do this. I hug Jannah and Momma takes her.

"Pam. This baby is loved and will be looked after. You know that. Now you go ahead and do good for the both of you. Go on and hold your head up high. I love you."

Marcus is parked on the street waiting and drives me to the bus station.

I leave Memphis.

Getting Established

Two weeks ago today I arrived in Phoenix. It is 111 degrees. The city is spread out and the sun is blinding bright. Yards here are a combination of grass, cactus and other desert plants.

I miss Jannah and the family to the point each day I think about returning to Memphis and consider this an extended vacation. The separation doesn't feel normal. I speak to Jannah daily and Momma says I need to give it more time.

Georgia left out one minor detail with this new move. There are no black people. I go for days and barely see anyone who looks like me. Memphis music was a luxury undoubtedly I took for granted. She listens to soft rock and country. If Georgia buys a cowboy hat I'll leave.

She resides in a rather large three-bedroom house in northwest Phoenix. She and her four daughters live comfortably off her deceased husband's social security and so far she is not interested in working. Her youngest daughter, Mariah, and Jannah are the same age. Mariah will have a playmate when she arrives.

Early mornings before it becomes unbearably hot, Georgia drives me around to submit applications. After today's job search, her oldest daughter, Reba had taken a message from someone at Mountain Bell regarding a job. How can this be? I filled out the application three days ago. I return the call.

Mountain Bell has several openings in their repair service bureau. They would like for me to take a two-hour test this Friday at eight-thirty. All applicants passing will be interviewed shortly afterwards.

I phone Momma and ask everyone on her end to pray all will go well for me. Jannah is not there. Melinda took her for ice cream. If I don't locate a job in at least two more weeks I am heading for home.

Today is the test day. The test center is located downtown and Georgia knows exactly where it is. The building is red brick and nondescript with white company vehicles in a gated rear parking lot. A McDonald's restaurant is across the street, and Georgia and Mariah will wait there for me.

As I enter, a security guard asks me to sign in and checks my driver's license. He instructs me to go to the third floor. An easel holding a sign with an arrow points down the hall for applicant testing as I exit the elevator. Inside the test room a young Hispanic lady is sitting in front. She politely instructs everyone entering to take a seat. There is a pencil and blank sheet of paper on each school-type desk.

At eight twenty-five the lady explains the test sections and encourages us to use the blank sheet for the mathematics portion if necessary. We are to wait in a lounge down the hall after completing the test. Eight-thirty we begin and at nine-fifty I am finished.

It is ten forty-five and all the applicants are eagerly waiting in the designated lounge. A few smokers are gathered in a corner talking. A man enters the room and calls out a name. It isn't mine. Minutes later, a woman enters the room and my name is called. Evidently I passed.

This lady is actually a supervisor at the repair service bureau. She explains the history of Mountain Bell and Arizona's unique rural communities. The company is seeking individuals to provide excellent customer service in her department. Lastly, pay and benefits. When the twenty-five-minute interview ends, we shake hands. She asks after references are checked and if I am offered a position, what is my availability? I respond, immediately. I dare not become overly excited. There are at least thirty applicants here for three positions.

I walk across to McDonald's and Georgia is watching Mariah as she plays in the fun gym. I am famished. She is positive I will be hired after I give her the details of the interview.

At five-fifteen I receive a call from Mountain Bell's human resources. I am offered a job and I gladly accept. Training for one week begins Monday from seven-thirty to four in the same building I tested in. I officially go to work the following week.

"Thank you Lord! Georgia I got the job and start training on Monday. Monday! Can you believe this! Now I can make plans to send for Jannah. Thank you for taking me there this morning, waiting and everything."

"Pam, you are welcome. How many people can go to a new city and land a job this quickly? A good job by the way. You were at the right place at the right time."

I phone home with the good news and Momma has a much more gratifying surprise. They had planned to fly Jannah to Arizona upon my request. She will be here next month. We celebrate tonight by preparing a nice Mexican dinner with homemade burritos, guacamole, rice, and beans.

The first couple of mornings Georgia took me to training and midweek I began riding the bus. Her older model vehicle simply can't make the regular distance. The new job is located about five miles from the training center on the same bus route and it stops directly in front of the building.

Three weeks later

The new job and all is falling into place. Tomorrow evening Jannah will be here. An oversized box arrived Tuesday with her toys and clothes. It is still considerably hot here and I bought a few new cool outfits for her. I will pay Georgia a small fee to watch Jannah while I work.

Saturday evening

Jannah's flight arrives at six-thirty. Georgia, Mariah, and I are the first to arrive. We wanted to allow time for any unforeseen situation. I bought her an adorable brown teddy bear. I can't sit still so I look anxiously out at the terminal and I see the plane taxiing in. Georgia looks at me and says, only a few more minutes, Pam.

As the attendant opens the door for the passengers to exit, Jannah and the flight attendant are the first to appear. She notices me and breaks away from the lady holding her hand. Look at my beautiful little angel. She screams as soon as she spots me,

"Mommy. Mommy."

"Hey baby. Hey Jannah."

I start to cry. She is finally in my arms again and I now feel complete. We will never be separated again. Never.

Jannah is dressed in a darling pink ruffled pantsuit and a pink bow in her hair. She is carrying a blanket and her baby doll. The attendant is rolling her little Strawberry Shortcake luggage.

The attendant asks for my identification and we laugh. She says I must follow the rules but you are certainly Jannah's mom. Jannah is speaking clearly and looks taller. She was asleep during the last few hours of the flight and the attendant escorting her said during the entire flight she behaved as though she travels regularly. Jannah waves at Georgia and Mariah and insists I hold her. And I do, all the way to the house.

While waiting for a pizza to arrive, I call my parents to let them know she is safe in my arms again. Jannah continues to sit on my lap even while becoming familiar with Mariah and her siblings. Jannah and I will be sharing the room with her oldest daughter. I purchased a cot and extra items for us to be comfortable.

Sunday

Today is bonding time. We lounged around and Jannah and Mariah finally played together. I may not be in a

church today but I am thankful for so many blessings.
Amen.

Monday

Today is day one I leave Jannah to go to work. I feel horrible she has only been here less than two days and now I must leave her. I have no choice other than to return back to Memphis but I will give Phoenix a fair chance to work.

I call on the first break and Georgia says she cried and asked for me when she got up but soon afterwards she calmed down. Jannah, Mommy is trying to make it work for us.

The Arizona sun is mercilessly scorching, but I am too happy earning money to complain about walking four blocks home in the evenings. Tomorrow I will take an umbrella to guard myself from the sun and minimize perspiring as much.

Walking home I notice several of the homes with tea bags brewing naturally in huge jars of water in the sun on their porches. I miss Jannah something terrible and I am eager to see how her and Mariah's day went.

Georgia placed the sofa at the living room window for the girls to look out and as I near the house Jannah calls out to me. I wave to let her know I hear her sweet little voice. She darts out of the house and I immediately notice a bandage on her arm. Before I can speak one word, she is going on about Mariah scratching her. I kiss her and the bandage.

Georgia is in the kitchen preparing burgers and fries. I am hot and my clothes are drenched with perspiration. I sit down at the kitchen table and get a bag from my purse. I have cookies for Mariah and Jannah.

"Georgia, what happened to Jannah's arm? And, I hope you don't mind if I give Mariah a cookie. We had a celebration at work and there were lots of sweets left over."

"She can have a cookie, Pam. Mariah will eat when she gets hungry. I am sorry Mariah scratched Jannah. Mariah was trying to get Jannah to go with her and when Jannah pulled away Mariah accidentally scratched her."

"Oh, okay. Georgia we are going to have to do something about these roaches. They are out of control and there are lots of them here in the kitchen. Doesn't it get on your nerves?"

"Pam, yes they bother me. But I can only do so much. I kill them every chance I get. I can't do a lot of spraying, it will cause my asthma to flare."

"I understand but I am afraid one of the girls may pick up a toy or something after one of those bugs has been on it. That would be terrible."

"I've thought about that, Pam."

"Georgia, Friday why don't we get spray, gloves, and disinfectant and see if we can get rid of them? At least the majority of them."

"Sounds like a plan to me."

Roaches are in every room of this house. Georgia had this same problem in Memphis but not to this degree. I am paranoid one will find its way inside one of our babies' ears as they nap.

Friday will not arrive soon enough.

The Horror of House Cleaning

Tonight we are going to battle this infestation of roaches. I am literally miserable and deeply concerned about the girls' health. We went to the store and purchased the items to get started. Everywhere I turn one of those filthy creatures appears. They are in the kitchen sink, on the wall over the stove, and I sat on the sofa earlier and one crawled over me. That was a breaking point and I insisted we go into "annihilation mode." I am terrified that somehow they will figure out a way to get into the refrigerator. These seem as though they congregate without fear of being killed. This has to cease.

For dinner tonight, I placed several chicken pot pies in the oven and after they began to cook, the oven reeked with a strange odor. I asked Georgia what it was and she did not know. It was an awful stench that made me sick to my stomach. Something other than the food is cooking and I don't want to think about it. I am hungry for a snack but I dare not eat anything from the cupboards outside of a box for fear of roach contamination. The Jell-o snacks and fruit for the girls are kept in the refrigerator. Lord help us!

The plan is to have everyone settled in the living room while Georgia and I kill and disinfect the kitchen first. We will take turns spraying and the other will sweep them out the back door. While we are spraying down the side of the stove and refrigerator, this infestation is unbelievable.

It is far worse than we had imagined and the roaches are coming out faster than we can kill them. We both panic and begin to scream and jump out of the kitchen. Mariah starts crying and Jannah follows. Georgia's eldest daughter is consoling the both of them and her other daughters are laughing. This is the epitome of domestic madness.

"Georgia, this is over our heads. What are we going to do?"

"Wait. I have an idea. Amber, go get the vacuum and get the hose attachment. Pam. It's too many of them."

"Girl, you have got to be kidding. Use the vacuum. This is absurd. Lord have mercy!"

"Amber, hurry up!" she screamed.

Georgia tied a diaper around her face to cover her nose and mouth. She sprayed the bugs and I vacuumed. This is a scene from a horror film. The sound of the roaches clicking and clacking into the vacuum sounds more like popcorn. Several minutes pass and oddly they keep coming from behind the refrigerator. We stop.

"Pam. We need to pull the refrigerator out. They keep coming and going to the back of it."

"Okay, let's do this."

She slowly begins pulling the refrigerator away from the wall and we both become hysterical. They are layered on the wall and coils of the refrigerator. This is the mother lode of roach filth. The spraying and vacuuming goes on for a little while longer and eventually we are done with the kitchen.

"Georgia, I will never forget this as long as I live."

"You! Girl, I need a cigarette behind all this."

She lights a cigarette and suggests we rest awhile before we tackle the rest of the house. Reba had taken Mariah and Jannah in the back away from the lingering smell. The sad truth to this horrifying evening is this infestation originated from Memphis. This six-legged tribe traveled in a U-haul to Phoenix. Georgia has the heart of a saint and literally will give you the "clothes off her back" but she falls short with her domestic ambitions. The fumes and activity caused her asthma to flare terribly. This was it for one night.

After this incident, I know I can no longer live with Georgia. I have minimum tolerance when it comes to unsanitary conditions. We need prayer.

Monday

It is five forty-five in the morning and I am softly walking with sandals through the house in an effort to avoid stepping on anything crawling and to not wake anyone, especially Jannah. My shift begins at seven-thirty and I can't miss the seven o'clock bus. I plug in the iron and gather a white skirt and pink chiffon top. With everyone asleep getting ready should be simple and fast.

When I return from washing-up and combing my hair I have twenty minutes to head out the door. Quickly ironing the skirt, it begins to soil. Oh no! The iron is dirty. I unplug the iron and take it and the skirt to the bathroom. What in the world is this smell coming from? I close the bathroom door and as I turn on the light I scream and drop the iron. Those filthy nasty roaches had somehow got into the iron and I scorched one on my clean white skirt. I sit on the edge of the tub and cry. I can't take this. God please help me!

I should have known better than to iron white clothes before checking to see if the iron was clean. It is too late to search for another outfit. Five long minutes I sit to recompose myself and focus, knowing full well this cuts into my preparation time. I take a deep breath and wash the soiled section with soap and water. With no desire to iron, I put the wrinkled skirt and top on and leave.

I have been living with Georgia for almost a couple of months now trying to disinfect and destroy. I need a plan to take Jannah and me out of this. I am not better than Georgia but I want to live better. No, live cleaner. God provided me with a job one week after arriving here and he will certainly give me answers. Jannah and I did not relocate to the other side of the country to be unhappy. I catch the bus in time and I peer out the window thinking.

After my first cup of coffee I sit in my work cubicle and decide to write down a plan. A solid plan to get us on our own or I am eventually going to lose it. During lunch I walk to the corner Circle K and purchase a paper to see what the rentals are going for in the area. My pay is pretty much the same every two weeks and this will provide me with a starting point as to what I can afford.

I have forty-five minutes for lunch and today I plan to visit the daycare, Little Round-up. It is one block west of my job. Yes, I need a place to stay and someone other than Georgia to watch Jannah.

I am reading and walking swiftly to Little Round-up trying to stay on top of time. As I enter the little white gate I see toddlers playing in the sandbox and swings having a good time. A really young girl approaches me. I tell her I want some information on her daycare and I work at Mountain Bell. She takes me inside and introduces me to an older woman, Mrs. Baxter, who is her mother. She gives me a tour of the facility, daily schedule, and finally, the fees. The fees are higher than I expected but I will make this work. The facility is clean and has a structured program. Mrs. Baxter hands me with a huge information packet to fill out and reiterates she only has a couple of openings and not to wait too long to make a decision. How convenient it would be to work, locate an apartment, and place Jannah in a daycare in walking distance.

I spend the entire afternoon circling apartments in the area. Some are furnished. I use the phone in the employee lounge to make calls. Will Georgia understand if I tell her the bugs are too much to live with? She will be seriously offended for certain. I get paid next weekend and that will at least give me time to figure out daycare and living expenses.

The afternoon is here and it is time for me to head out. I am able to stand inside the building and see the bus approaching. This works in my favor especially when it rains or it is too hot. The bus drivers are accustomed to employees exiting the building and they reduce their speeds as they approach the stop. I appreciate these small blessings.

I bid the bus driver farewell and open my umbrella. All of this walking back and forth is causing me to lose weight rapidly. I can't afford to buy any new clothes and I think I am looking a little sloppy.

A horn blows and Georgia pulls up beside me. What a welcome surprise.

"Hey Pam! Come one and get in."

"What are you doing out in this heat?"

"I went to the store."

"Thank you. You know I appreciate this."

"Mommy! Mommy!" Jannah is excited jumping up and down. She and Mariah are eating freeze pops.

When I put my things on the floor and turn around to give her a hug I see a large, long scratch on her right cheek and it is deep.

"Georgia, what happened to my baby's face? How did she get scratched up like that?"

Georgia senses right away I am livid.

"Mariah and Jannah were playing a little rough and as you know when children play, things happen from time to time."

"From time to time! Georgia, it seems every time I look around Jannah is constantly getting marked up or scratched and Mariah never has a mark or scratch on her!"

Georgia does not say a word. We pull up in the drive and I pick Jannah up and kiss her face. I go directly to the back room to see if I can locate a more effective medicine to put on it. If I don't medicate this wound it will be on her pretty little face for life. This scratch is deep. It is enough she has a small one from my caesarean.

We are in the room alone for most of the night. Georgia and I never have disagreements or exchange words. I don't care. Right is right. This is the third incident and each time Mariah is unharmed. Jannah is being treated unfairly or Georgia is not closely monitoring our babies. Jannah is light-skinned and facial flaws may have a negative impact on her self esteem as she gets older. The mere idea saddens me.

Scarring on the face is very personal to me. No, it is more than personal. I have major issues with scarring faces. When I was thirteen years old I was playing hop-scotch with my sister Stephanie in our front drive. Another thirteen-year-old girl who lived on Eloise was apparently jealous of me. It was that "dark skin–light skin" thing. She literally attacked me from behind and I lost my balance. I tried to fight her off but somehow she ended up sitting on top of me and carved the initial of her first name on my left cheek. That little incident caused me to become introverted during those teen years and I saw myself as unattractive. Aunt Bell said they were fortunate we are Christians or there would have been consequences for that girl's intention to destroy my face. By the grace of God Almighty, and Aunt Bell and Momma's cocoa butter–like homemade remedies, the scar diminished. Today, you can only see the remnants of that despicable incident if you look extremely close.

I do not know how to deal with Georgia so I decide to

refrain from any contact. I bathe Jannah and when I am powdering her down Georgia comes into the room.

"Pam, dinner is ready. Aren't you and Jannah going to eat?"

"I am not hungry but I will get a little something for Jannah. Thanks."

Georgia sits on the bed and takes a deep sigh. "Pam, I am sorry Mariah scratched Jannah. Mariah apologized and I had her hug Jannah. You only have one child and I have four. These types of things happen all the time when kids play. You are a tad overprotective and again this is because you only have one."

"Georgia, you couldn't be more wrong. Whether I had seven like my mother I seriously believe I would feel the same way."

"I don't know what to tell you. Mariah is territorial but I am teaching her she has to share. Pam, if you feel that strongly about her under my care, maybe you need to have someone else watch her if you don't trust me."

"Georgia it's not that I don't trust you. That's not the issue. Let's not talk about it anymore. I will be out in a minute."

She leaves the room.

Well, God, I asked for guidance and now I have an answer. It is time for Jannah and me to leave. Whenever I am here nothing happens. Nothing! While I am combing Jannah's hair, a roach crawls across the wall. You and your friends can stay here because we are leaving. I look at Jannah and say, "Mommy did not come this far for this. No way! No how!"

The mere thought of the possibility of these roaches

in contact with Jannah and Mariah's toys makes me nauseous.

I iron another skirt and blouse and do not mention to Georgia about my morning. I hang them up over the door as a precaution.

God, you guided me across country and blessed me with a new good job and possibly a close daycare. I trust you and thank you ahead for the blessings. I believe in my heart you have found Jannah and me another place to live. I only need to get to it. I must also remember we are covered by my parents' and Aunt Bell's prayers. Who knows, maybe Jassem's?

God, why is it each and every time I am faced with these situations I incessantly think about Jassem. I wonder how he is living.

Surely, not like this.

Truly On Our Own

I do not sleep well. I am afraid a roach will crawl over Jannah as she sleeps. Again, this is insanity. Before leaving I kiss her and silently pray over her. God please protect her and absolutely no physical harm come to her.

Good grief! Ten minutes to catch this bus and I haven't made it to the corner. I remove my one-inch-heel shoes and start running. I finally make it to the corner across from the bus stop and it drives past. I wave and wave frantically. The driver recognizes me and waits. I can hardly breathe and I thank him. The bus is cold, empty, and I take a front window seat and rest my head on the glass.

If it were not for my job I would probably be heading back to Memphis. I have got to give this a chance. This does not rise to the level of surrendering, only repositioning.

Walking into the building I see a co-worker, Darlene. She is from Brooklyn, New York, and has every bit of the accent to prove it. She is curious as to where I reside and is surprised to learn I live so far from work. I ask her to keep an eye out for me on a new place to live. She recommends specific areas near the job. Darlene is quite encouraging and offers to assist me in any way. I may need her assistance when the time arrives. Between calls I search the newspaper incessantly. I am determined to find somewhere nearby.

At lunch I phone several advertisements and two are reasonable. One is furnished and what does furnished exactly mean? I am too embarrassed to ask anyone. I don't know anything about apartment living. At this point, sleeping bags will be a welcome improvement for Jannah and me. I tell one gentleman with the furnished apartment I will contact him later to make an appointment to see the one-bedroom. I need to figure out where and how to get there. I only know it is on this side of town. Maybe I am moving too fast here and not really thinking things clearly through. Maybe I can schedule an appointment right after work or the weekend.

During an afternoon break I take the daycare packet back to Little Round-up. Everything is now in order for Jannah to begin Monday after next. Jannah and I will be fine riding the bus together. She is going to make new friends and be happy here. And to think I am only a block away.

Today is the busiest day so far since I've been working here. Repair call after call. Marguarite, my supervisor, walks over to my cube and praises me on how calmly I handle customers. Does she have the right employee? She is going to recommend I begin training on the "irate desk." This is a department where unsatisfied or irate customers are transferred. It is a lateral move.

Another scorcher walking home! I hope there aren't any problems today. Getting closer to the house Jannah and Mariah are in the window waving excitedly like clockwork. Motherhood is so wonderful. At the end of a day and dealing with the challenges of life, your babies can lift your blues. Georgia opens the door and all appears well. No bumps, bruises or cuts.

She is in a jovial mood and hands me two letters – one from Momma and Vanessa. Jannah is so filled with joy to see me she will not allow me to put her down. No Jassem, grandfather, grandmother, uncles, or aunts to spoil her. I am it! This sweet little angel deserves my best. Momma sent me a beautiful card with fifty dollars. Yes, I can take this to Little Round-up for the fifty-dollar registration fee. It is lonesome not being able to walk over to friends or sit at the coffee shop with Vanessa. I miss my Memphis. No need to have a pity party. This is the ultimate price you pay when moving five states over by yourself.

Until I am certain of the apartment outcome I will not mention anything to Georgia regarding moving out. However, I will need to tell her about the daycare. Our family regards her as a dear friend and we know this is not what anyone had in mind. I love Georgia and ideally would like to remain here but this is no longer about our friendship. I made a conscious choice to leave Memphis and this is part of the responsibility.

Friday

I am to meet a Mr. Harold Helwig and his wife after work to see their property on 32nd Street. I am taking my $100 emergency fund just in case. I told Georgia I needed to make a stop after work and to expect me a little later.

I along with several other people exit the bus and need to transfer. The buses are lined up waiting for passengers across the street. Now I need to make certain to get on the right bus, number 18. Yes, here it is. I hand the transfer to the driver and ask would he please let me know when I am near Locust Street and he nods yes. There is a huge busy supermarket and Walgreens across from the bus stop – how convenient. Adobe homes and palm trees with desert landscape fill the neighborhood. This bus is stopping at every block.

"Miss, here's Locust Street."

"Thank you."

He tells me to cross the street and go four blocks down and I would be there, 29th Street. Yipes! Four blocks! Not again. The neighborhood is quiet, older and well maintained. There are large swamp coolers, not the air conditioners people have in Memphis. Here is 29th Street. Mr. Helwig said a red-and-white for-rent sign would be in the front of the apartments. An older white gentleman is watering the property and there is a for-rent sign in front.

"Hi. I am looking for Mr. Helwig."

"Hi, I am he! You must be Pam. Nice to meet you."

"Nice to meet you too, sir!"

He places the water hose inside the front flower bed. We walk inside the court and turn left into apartment number one. It is the first on the left. There are a total of six units – three on the right and three on the left. In the center of the court is a small palm bush decorated with desert plants. All of the apartments have screen doors and I love this amenity. This makes for a fresh breeze to flow through.

"I like to keep the property green and clean."

We walk inside the apartment and it smells of fresh paint. Everything looks brand new. All of the windows open out unlike the ones back home that rise up and down. There is a large double window to the left and a brown-and-white plaid couch with a loveseat and nice end tables on the right – old fashioned but nevertheless clean. There is also a large swamp cooler in one of the living room windows.

"There is brand new carpeting throughout the place and fresh paint as you can tell. How many are in your family?"

"Just my two-year old daughter and me."

"How soon are you needing a place?"

"Right away."

"Well, take a look around. I am going to my car to get an application."

The kitchen is white and yellow with a window over the sink. The view is partially blocked by a tree but you can clearly see the street. There is a small steel and red dinette. The back door has a double lock and a screen as well. A small clothesline is directly outside the back door. I open the door and take a peek. It looks like all the units have clotheslines. The yard is separated by a brick wall and tall trees. So you can open your kitchen door with privacy. I open all the cabinets and there are a few odds-and-ends dishes. There is a small old-fashioned refrigerator like Aunt Bell's and it is clean too! Exiting the kitchen to the left is the bedroom and bath.

The bedroom has a full-size bed with a dresser with a mirror and night stand. There is a chest at the foot of the bed. Jannah can begin to collect her toys in there. The furniture is wood with a deep dark brown stain. The bathroom is a light pink and white. Not a crawling or flying anything in sight. This is perfect. Jannah can play in the front.

"Pam. Here is the application. Do you want to take it with you or fill it out now?"

"I want to fill it out now if it's okay with you."

"Well, Pam, we've had the property for about seven years and it was time to replace some things. My wife picked out the furniture and curtains. I am looking to rent this out right away. I have some others interested. You are the last one I am going to show it to. What do you think? You want to make this home for you and your baby?"

"I hope so. I was thinking my daughter could play outside in the front."

"There is a young fellow who lives in number six with a two-year-old son. He's a widower. His wife passed away last year. What a shame! Where do you work?"

"I work for Mountain Bell. This would be my first apartment."

"Well, I need someone to move in right away."

I sit down on the couch and use the coffee table to fill out the two-sided application. Mr. Helwig sits in one of the dinette chairs and patiently waits. I hand it back to him.

"Oh, you are a newcomer to the area. You moved here and got a good job with Mountain Bell right away. Young lady, you are lucky!"

"Well the rent is $285 and the deposit is $75. We ask for a higher deposit because of all the new furniture, carpet and things. I will prorate the $285 since it is the middle of the month. So let me see. I need at least $200 to hold the apartment."

I only had $100 cash and I need the $50 Momma sent for daycare. I need to tell him something and quick. I don't get paid for another week.

"Mr. Helwig I really like the place and I want to rent it. I have $100 cash and I can give you the rest on next Friday, which is a payday for me."

"I don't know. I have other people who can pay today and move in tomorrow. I need to discuss it with the wife. Give me a call tomorrow around 9:00 a.m. and I will let you know. You can't write me a post-dated check to at least hold it?"

"Like I said, Mr. Helwig, I have cash."

"Well, I would hate to see you not get the place. There is a 7-Eleven down the street to your left that sells money orders. I don't take cash. I will hold the place for you with the $100."

"I will be right back."

I purchase a money order and I am back within a few minutes. Mr. Helwig is watering the lawn again.

"Here you are, Mr. Helwig."

"I spoke with my wife and she seems to be okay with everything."

"Are you serious? Thank you, Mr. Helwig."

"I forgot to show you the laundry room and parking area."

I hadn't given thought to washing clothes. We walk directly behind the last apartment in the rear to a locked laundry room facing the alley. There is a window on the door probably used to allow some of the heat to escape when drying. Inside this small area are a full-size washer and dryer with an industrial sink. Laundry detergents line a shelf above the washer. These items must belong to some of the tenants. A gravel parking lot is at the end of the court with an official private parking sign posted.

"Most of the tenants leave their washing powder here. You can pay me $245 next Friday and I will meet you here with the keys."

No, this man did not say give me the keys. An elderly woman slowly walks up and Mr. Helwig introduces her.

"Mrs. Blanche, this is Pam. She and her little girl will be renting number one. Mrs. Blanche keeps an eye on things around here. She will be your next door neighbor."

Mrs. Blanche offers assistance if I need anything. She is feeble and trembles. She takes care of an aging husband who is bedridden for the most part. It is difficult to imagine her taking care of anyone. She looks as though she requires assistance herself.

Mr. Helwig and I will meet the same time next Friday. No need to rush. The next bus will not be there for another 20 minutes. I have an apartment. I can't believe this. Thank the Lord for giving me enough sense to bring the $100 with me!

It is almost seven o'clock. I walk through the door and the house is empty. I am exhausted but too excited to allow anything to make me feel pooped. Where is everyone? Georgia left a note on the dining room table. At six-thirty they left to go to a neighborhood carnival. This will give me some quiet time to shower and place my thoughts on paper. I turn off the swamp cooler and open the back and front doors.

After showering I take a chair out to the carport. I now have a moment to reflect and take in the day. One thing Georgia and I do have in common is being keen fans of Elton John. She has all his eight-tracks. His music and this warm Arizona breeze are surreal.

Jassem! Where are you? Here I go again. How can I break this habit when those addictive memories haunt my peace? Had we married as planned Jannah would see us together every day in a clean and loving home. Probably pregnant with our second or even third child and surely not sitting here thinking about money. If only one day, I open the door and see him standing there, I would fall in love with him again.

I have not set foot in a church since leaving home. Even though I pray to God, it is not the same as being at church. There has to be a Church of Christ in the area. When I get settled I am going to locate a congregation. I can really use some good ministering and singing. Daddy would be relieved to know I found a congregation and placed my membership. Besides, there is no way I am going to raise Jannah without the Lord. No way. Talk about horrible. What else would sustain her with life's uncertainties?

It is close to sunset when Georgia and the girls drive up singing with the radio. Yes, it appears they had a pretty good outing. Jannah is excited for me to pick her up. I open the door and she bounces in my arms. Jannah and Mariah both began to babble away. I can't make sense out of neither one of them. I thank Georgia for taking Jannah to the carnival. She said they had ridden Shetland ponies and thought the traveling carnival was overpriced.

Afterwards she drove all around the neighborhood to see what is further northwest.

"Pam, two blocks over is the elementary school and a few yards down is a daycare. The girls are old enough to attend. So, if sometime in the future I go back to work part-time there are options. And, I found another daycare not too far from here in the opposite direction."

"Thanks, Georgia. I appreciate knowing all of this."

Was it that noticeable? I decide to share my plans with her. She does not seem the least surprised. The unsanitary conditions are deplorable; however, as a guest or tenant in her house I have no right to judge her so harshly. I am saddened we cannot live together; in spite of this, we will remain friends.

Rajean's Death

Phoenix has beautiful warm winters and this February evening epitomizes this reality. Jannah and I are happily settling into our new life and apartment. I have been working at Mountain Bell for several months now meeting new people from all over the country. Being able to bid successfully for first shift at work and conveniently enroll Jannah at Little Round-up is a huge blessing. The supermarket is located at the transfer stop and during the week sometimes I purchase a few items and on weekends do the full shopping. We have a nice little routine in place for newcomers to this desert city.

I had prepared lasagna, salad, and garlic bread for Sunday's dinner and there is more than enough for leftovers tonight. Jannah is playing in the tub while I set the table listening to Barry Gibb and Barbara Streisand. Afterwards, I plan to create a list of guests for her upcoming third birthday. The telephone rings and it is Momma.

"Hi Momma. I am glad you called. You must be missing us to call through the week."

"Pam you need to sit down. I have some really bad news," she says in a sorrowful tone.

I stop breathing and cautiously sit down to hear.

"Rajean is dead."

"Rajean is dead! What? No, Momma, this can't be true. How? Was she in a car accident?"

"No, Pam. She stood in front of her mother's house yesterday evening and shot herself."

There is dead silence between Momma and me. We both begin to cry.

"Momma, I will not even ask you how everyone is doing?"

"Not good. Her dad is taking it hard. I mean very hard."

"Momma, I don't feel good right now. I need to go and check on Jannah. I'll call you back later. Love you."

"I love you too. Kiss my baby for me."

My head begins to spin. I feel faint and sick to my stomach – I fall to the floor. Jannah is calling for me repeatedly but a lump in my throat prevents me from speaking. I am physically weak and I cannot seem to gain balance to stand. I literally crawl on hands and knees to the bathroom, continually falling over. Finally, I reach the bathroom and sit up on the side of the tub.

"Mommy's funny. Crawling like a kitty? Mommy! Why are you crying?"

"Remember Rajean who came to see us all the time. Well she is gone away and I will never see her again."

"Never mommy? Don't be sad mommy. Don't be sad mommy. I will help you."

I tightly hug and lift my little angel from the tub and she in turn takes the towel and begins to wipe my tears, bringing comfort and a somber smile to me.

Later that night I call Momma. Rajean was obsessed

with having the need to attend worship at our church yesterday. With no obvious transportation, earlier in the day she spoke of a neighbor promising to take her to evening service – unfortunately, this lady never called or arrived. Rajean apparently waited diligently on the front porch steps beyond nightfall. Perhaps, this simple mission of hope was her last stance to survive.

Sunday evening the family was watching television and a popping sound occurred. They assumed the noise to be a truck backfiring. Peculiarly, Auntie, giving it a second thought, sent someone to the door to check it out.

She was lying in the front yard face down, head immersed in blood.

Rajean!

Rajean!

Sunday, February 8, 1982.

Life in Arizona

I purchase a 1966 Chevrolet Impala for $150 from a co-worker at Mountain Bell. The freedom to drive Jannah and me where and when I choose is exhilarating.

The tenant in apartment #5 moved out and a single mother, Rosalyn, with a teenage son is moving in. Jannah is playing in the front with her dolls and wagon as I watch out the window. A woman assisting Rosalyn with the move approaches Jannah and I walk out. Her name is Joyce and her husband Jonathan is a youth minister at the local Church of Christ. To think this meeting easily could have been a lost opportunity. Earlier I planned to take Jannah to the park and something compelled me to stay at home.

Joyce and I talk for two hours. The church is ten minutes away from where I live and we exchange phone numbers. I invite Joyce and her husband over for dinner Sunday after service. I pour my heart out to her about the disconnection of not having a church family and how I so yearn to fill this void.

Sunday morning I bake chicken and cabbage and make a salad before leaving to locate the small congregation in south Phoenix. It is exactly how Joyce described it – a brown adobe building on the southwest corner. The parking lot is across the street from the church. Jannah and I are both dressed in pink. The young adult morning bible class is in session and the minister, Brother Turner, is teaching. We sit quietly in the back row and observe. Soon Joyce walks in and joins us. After class I meet her husband, relatives, and fellow members.

Two weeks later I place my membership at the Tonto Street Church of Christ. Jannah enjoys Sunday school and Wednesday bible class. The joy of worshiping with fellow Christians is an indescribable bond.

God thank you for all the blessings you have bestowed upon me since leaving Memphis. Jannah and I are truly blessed.

Six months later

Today two of my friends, Danielle and Bernadette, from church are meeting me at the local mall to go shopping. I am to meet them in J.C. Penney's near the children's department escalator.

Bernadette is from Chicago, Illinois. She is sophisticated, single, and her attractiveness causes men to continually annoy her.

Danielle is also an attractive newlywed from Tulsa, Oklahoma, who speaks her mind and frequently has us stunned and laughing at the outrageous tales of her social life in Tulsa. She wears her hair short and it is perfectly cut – never a strand out of place. She has three children and the youngest is near Jannah's age.

Her husband is from Phoenix and they met during

a singles conference. His parents wasted no time telling anyone who listened about Danielle not being forthright with divulging the truth as to how many children she actually had until after marriage. An annulment loomed but never materialized.

Danielle waves and gets my attention. Jannah and I walk over to the toddler area. Aisha, her youngest, and Bernadette are browsing through clothes. This sale has caused a crowd of bargain shoppers. Bernadette has no children but she shops for a niece back east.

I select three summer outfits and place them against Jannah for fitting. The items look darling. Bernadette has a couple of dresses for her infant niece. I add four dresses for church to purchase. Danielle stops and peers at the items in my arms.

"Pam, are you going to buy all those clothes? Don't you think that's enough?"

"Yes, I am buying play and church outfits for Jannah. You know me. I want her to look like a little princess every Sunday."

"Why do you always think your baby is better than everybody else?"

"Excuse me?"

"You think Jannah is better than everyone."

"No I don't. I only want her to be a well-maintained little girl. What's wrong with you? Why would you say something like that to me anyway?"

"I call them as I see them and you think your baby is better. By the way, there is nothing wrong with me."

"I only have the one to spoil and I will."

"What do you mean by that?"

"Ladies, please let's talk about something else!" Bernadette said nervously.

"Wait a minute Bernadette. Danielle, no one stuck a gun to your head when you had your three children. Oh and by the way, I work and spend my money as I please."

"Oh that's it. I will come over there and whip your yellow behind."

"Danielle, I don't know what your problem is today but you are going to find yourself under those dresses behind you."

I push Jannah to the side and take my earrings off and place them in my purse. Bernadette stands in front of Danielle and extends her arms. Danielle furiously shouts, "Heifer, I will send you back to Memphis."

Danielle takes a step and Bernadette pushes her back and says with a louder voice, "Lord have mercy! We are all Christians here in the name of Jesus! Please!"

"See you have now called me out of my name twice. Danielle, if you raise up on me you will be in trouble."

"That's it. You are getting your butt whipped today."

Bernadette's nervousness is now borderline panic with repetitive shouts to the Lord. Jannah and Aisha are oblivious as to what is going on with their mothers. This is not happening. A pleasant day of shopping has escalated into a stinking cat fight and with a Christian from church. This is the lowest.

I gaze at Bernadette, shake my head, and take Jannah's hand and walk away, without so much as a gesture of leaving. Aisha and Jannah are saying good-bye and I take the escalator up. I pay for the items upstairs in the jewelry department and leave the mall.

If Danielle and I engaged in a physical brawl we could have easily been arrested, not to mention physically hurt one another. Second, what mother fights with her baby there? Dear God! Why must I continually be confronted by stupid, ill-willed silly women? In retrospect, I should have completely ignored Danielle.

God please forgive me for this one!

Marriage

(Intentionally left blank)

The Invasion of Kuwait

August 2, 1990, Saddam Hussein, President of Iraq, invades Kuwait. Over the years I incessantly maintained interest in the Middle East, especially Kuwait. This news is heartbreaking and immediately I think of Jassem, Latif, and others who are in the Kuwaiti Air Force. Is the infiltration far reaching into the residential areas where Jannah's unknown relatives and others reside? I pray for the Lord to expeditiously intervene.

Hours pass as I sit in the exact spot transfixed to the news. Jannah is sitting next to me on the sofa and softly asks for a postage stamp. I assume she is writing a letter to one of our relatives. I pass her a stamp from my purse and ask who is she writing and she responds, President Bush. She does not say why and I have the propensity to inquire but change my mind – we both know. At eleven years old, she is mature for her age and early on, I instilled the significance of being perspicaciously aware of world matters beyond one's own backyard.

Three weeks later

The White House sends Jannah an autographed photo

of President George H. W. Bush. Her compelling solemn correspondence asking our President to assist Kuwait had ended with a youthful request for a souvenir, as you can only imagine a child to do.

Through the Years

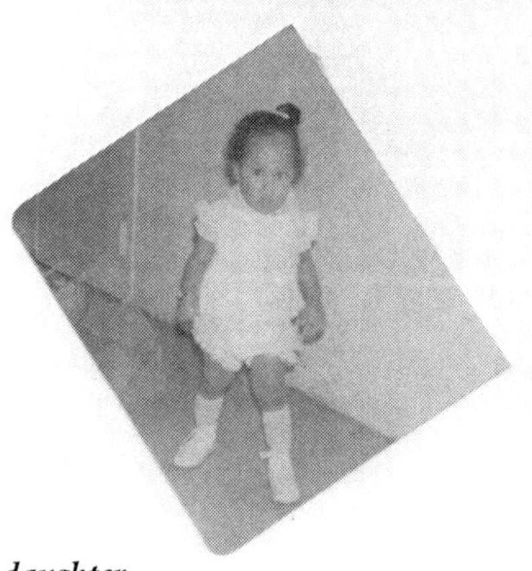

My daughter

A Spiritual Moment

Each moment in life must pass through the permissive will of God – for most this alone is beyond comprehension.

Through the trials and triumphs it was not until I was much older I began reflecting over circumstances to extract God's lessons for my life. In many instances I drew a conclusion to trust God, be obedient as best I can and know with an unwavering faith He is always with me, and most ordeals in life are never completely understood. (Ephesians 3:19: And to know the love of Christ, which passeth knowledge, that ye might be filled with all the fullness of God.)

God allowed me to make the best of choices and a few of the worst but always patiently loving me all the way. My life has never been even close to perfect but I am thankful to have the perfect will of God.

Praying!

One of the greatest blessings of my life has been the priceless power of prayer. Arising numerous times off my knees with confidence only our Heavenly Father can provide. During intense praying, pressure flees as I peel away painful burdens, personal and for others. (Matthew

11:28: Come unto me, all ye that labour and are heavy laden, and I will give you rest.)

There are times I laugh. Yes, laugh. Usually some circumstance I prayed about and the outcome without a shred of doubt was God's unmerited favor over me. I have been removed from situations, opportunities granted and closed, delay in matters, and persons removed and placed on my path. Some circumstances so far removed from comprehension that I categorize them as "unspeakable joys." They're between God and me and I need not share with anyone.

Oh the times I have sat in utter silence – words failed me. Depression, hurtfulness, and devastation had me in a state of brokenness. But, I am reminded in all of my praying (Romans 8:26): Likewise the Spirit also helpeth our infirmities: for we know not what we should pray for as we ought: but the Spirit itself maketh intercession for us with groanings which cannot be uttered. A few of God's strategies I have not understood or agreed with. However, because He sees horizons before they appear, I trust Him.

What a beautiful place to reach in one's life when you can say, "I enjoy praying."

I am truly thankful and blessed by God for this unusual path early in life which allowed me to meet Jassem – a Muslim and father of my eldest daughter.

Ever so often in life we hear stories, myths and unimaginable, fairy-like tales about the one infinite love – the love never forgotten, seldom if ever replaced and always remembered for what it was. Time, wealth, culture, distance, and yes religion bear no prominence once she has established herself.

For whatever reason when the love is no longer present allow me to share... Simply be thankful for the bestowed season of love. Allow the cherished memories to resonate joyously on the balcony of your heart and consider yourself one of the few truly blessed. (James 1:17: Every good gift and every perfect gift is from above, and cometh down from the Father of lights, with whom is no variableness, neither shadow of turning.)

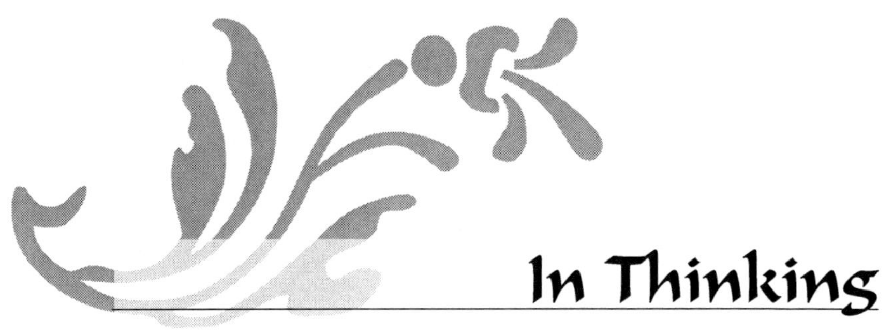

The coalescing of ignorance and hatred are perilous mind frames when poised at the forefront of any thought processes. It is as if an evil blind man uses a sword to guide him. The darkness of not only his human eyes but also his heart controls his spirit and, the damage he inflicts from the sword disturbs him not as he travels the path.

Somewhere in the world a Muslim loves a Christian and a Christian loves a Muslim. But equally as important, somewhere in the world a Muslim needlessly harbors hatred for a Christian and a Christian needlessly harbors hatred for a Muslim.

I cling to hope that Christians, non-Christians, and even perhaps those who are not of any religious belief will at the least be made aware of simple customs and beliefs Muslims practice. And, that Muslims and others acquire an understanding of Christians who follow the teachings of the church of Christ.

Today there is a generation of young Muslims emerging to dispel the negative traditions and ideologies as it relates to them as a people. I consciously through the years developed a sincere appreciation and an increasing understanding for Muslims – sharing always with many family, friends, and strangers a positive as well as truthful personal perspective as opposed to the damaging inundation of political quandaries on this subject.

It is a given that Muslims and Christians have numerous commonalities. However, it is greatly due again to ignorance, arrogance, and a crucial juncture of core beliefs that indeed separates us. The overwhelming majority of religious followers believe in the One True Living God. With whom most have faith, desire and anticipate the high honor of unification in an eternal life after death – believing this current short life as transitory.

Unfortunately, the means to paradise or heaven if you will is often complicated by man's own designs and not by God.

"If you seek to know a people you must go to the people."

Ms. Pamela
November 12, 2009

Breinigsville, PA USA
19 August 2010
243935BV00005B/54/P